MW01088736

Probate Real Estate Sales 101:

A guide for real estate agents and investors.

Tap into the $6 Trillion probate market and drive your financial numbers through the roof!!

By: Kevin Sayles

Contact Info: www.ProbateRealEstateSales101.com

Disclaimer

The purpose of this book is to help investors and real estate professionals understand the basics of the probate sale process. Neither the publisher nor author are engaged in providing advice of any type, especially financial, legal and tax advice. The information contained herein is considered accurate and was written based on the expertise of the author, a 20-plus year veteran in the industry. However, the information contained herein is not guaranteed. If legal, tax, or other advice is required, desired, or necessary, consult an appropriate, competent professional. Your results may vary from the examples, scenarios, and case studies presented. Names have been changed to protect confidentiality.

Furthermore, the author and publisher do not guarantee or warranty that any tips, techniques, suggestions, strategies, or ideas will apply to every situation. In probate and real estate in general, every situation is different and requires a different solution. Any place within this material where another organization, company or website is mentioned as a source for further information does not constitute an endorsement of such entity.

The reader acknowledges that some entities referenced within this material may be businesses affiliated with the author and/or publisher.

This material was written based on an understanding of probate and real estate procedures and probate law in the state of California. Many other states have similar rules and procedures, but there can be wide variance state by state. In fact, even within California, there may be procedural differences county by county. Check with your local governing body to ensure you are following local guidelines.

Thank you for purchasing this book.

I hope you enjoy it. This will be a great start on you increasing your knowledge about probate real estate. If you already are working in probate, this can be a great refresher and reference for you.

After reading this book please give us an authentic, genuine review in the place that you purchased it.

Thank you!

A portion of the profits from this book will be donated to a charity or non-profit that provides safe, clean housing in underserved communities.

Acknowledgements

I want to thank God for the things that I have learned over my career and been able to share in this book. I am thankful for my family. Thank you to my 4 boys for being the brightest joy in my life. Thank you to my parents for raising me to be a man. And most of all thank you to my wonderful wife…Darla.

Table of Contents

Foreword

You're out prospecting for listings or properties to buy, when a frazzled, brown haired fellow behind the millionth door you've knocked, abruptly cuts you off and says those words all agents want to hear: "Why YES! I'm glad you came to my door. I'm tired of this house and really NEED to sell it fast."

He's desperate, you're in the right place at the right time, and you're giddy with excitement.
But before you have a chance to invite yourself in and close the deal, our friend continues:

"Yes, Aunt Suzie passed a few years ago and she asked me to take care of her beloved home. My cousin George, who lives in Vermont, is Executor of the estate. We don't get along and I don't trust him. Either way, the property needs to be sold, and I should get half. That's what Aunt Suzie wanted. Can you help me?"

Will you be ready? Will you know what to say? Will you get the deal? Well, the answer should be "Yes!" because Kevin Sayles has written Probate Real Estate Sales 101 and it has all the information you need.

This book includes detailed information on the Probate process and the knowledge to market yourself in this niche. Additionally, there is a web-site with tons of tools to augment the book: probate timelines, sample attorney letters, probate listing checklists, etc. You have everything you need to flourish in the probate market.

I thank Kevin for putting this together. Probate is currently an important segment of the real estate market. I've known Kevin Sayles for two years and have benefited greatly from his probate knowledge and his overall marketing knowledge. He's been instrumental in helping me get my business and my office off the ground. He is a great person and a great business person and I'm thankful to have met him.

Hopefully, you take advantage of his book and material and look out for his next seminar!!

Dino Buiatti
Managing Partner – Nationwide Real Estate Executives
Los Angeles, California

Preface

I wrote this book for three reasons. The first reason I wrote this book is because I found a shortage of good understanding of the probate real estate sale process. There are many myths and urban legends that are believed to be true by the real estate community, the investing community and the public at large. I felt it was time to shatter them.

The second reason I wrote this book is that we are in the midst of the largest generational transfer of wealth from the baby boomers to the next generations. Now more than ever it is important to know the facts around probate, trusts and estates. As real estate professionals and investors, we will truly miss the biggest opportunity that has ever been placed before us if we do not take advantage of this time and opportunity to serve others as assets pass to the next generation.

The third reason I wrote this book is that I saw a gap in some of the probate material that has been published on the market. Some material is really good at describing the process, but not helping you market yourself. Other material is great at helping you market yourself, but not good at helping you understand how to close the transaction. I wanted this material to have it all. From start to finish, the goal here is for you to be able to deal with a probate transaction from lead, to check in the bank.

I come from a closing services background. I worked in banking for 6 years prior to working the last 16 years in title insurance. While an absolutely amazing real estate agent would be someone who closes 5 transactions per month, in the title industry I have been blessed to never close less than 30 transactions in a month. Back in the "glory years" (2001 to 2007) there were many years that I closed several hundred transactions every month. I bring this up not to brag, but rather to show the sheer volume of transactions that I have been involved in. I have seen almost everything!

The information in this book was not read somewhere, was not learned in some book of theory or the probate code books. I learned everything I know and put the information in this book all from my experience.

If you are brand new to probate real estate, I suggest you reference the glossary frequently so you understand terms being used. Remember, this book was written based on probate in California. Other states' procedures may differ slightly or vary widely, but the general idea of probate is the same. In fact, even here in California there can be procedural differences county by county or jurisdiction by jurisdiction (but the law is going to be the same statewide). Be sure to check with your local jurisdiction for specifics for your area.

Chapter 1 Understanding the Process

In order to understand probate real estate, we must first begin with the process. What is probate? What are the steps? Why should I work in probate real estate? You will discover the answers to these questions in this first chapter. In the subsequent chapters, we will cover the types of sales and the types of probates. Let's begin with what is probate:

Probate (the legal term for gathering the assets of a deceased person to pay his debts, and distributing the balance to his beneficiaries) is a court-supervised process which can span from several months to several years, depending upon the complexity of the case. Most probates close in less than two years, but almost all probates complete the three phases outlined on the following pages, no matter the length of time required.

I want to also cover some terms that I will be using quite often throughout this book:

Decedent- The person who passed away. The probate is filed for their estate.

Estate- The property and assets of an individual, including all real estate, bank accounts, life insurance policies, stocks and bonds and personal property.

Executor(male) Executrix(female)- The person or persons named in the will who will manage the estate of the decedent.

1

Administrator (male) Administratrix (female)- This person is appointed by the court to manage and oversee the court process for the estate of a decedent who has died without leaving a will.

Personal Representative- The person who is representing the estate. Often times they are referred to as the personal representative because they have not been appointed executor or administrator yet.

> *Note about these terms: Executor, administrator and personal representative (PR) are used throughout this book and are interchangeable for the most part. In a nutshell, these terms refer to the person in charge of the estate.*

Petitioner- The person that files for the probate. Often they end up being appointed either administrator or executor.

Beneficiary- The beneficiary is the person who receives property or other assets from a will, insurance policy, or contract.

Heir- A person legally entitled to the property of another on that person's death.

3 Phases of Probate

Recently, I helped a real estate agent establish massive rapport with the personal representative from a probate estate. There were two steps to the process and one is going to take up the bulk of this commentary. First, you have to have empathy. With the personal representative of the estate, you don't know what they're going through. They may have been very close to the decedent, there may be a lot of challenging issues with heirs, or beneficiaries or debtors, and you don't know what the circumstances are. So it is very important to have authentic, heartfelt empathy for what the person may be going through with the estate.

The second step is to keep frequent, open communication with the estate representative. I have heard countless times that the personal representative of the estate feels as though they don't know what's going on during the process. I have heard agents indicate that their client (the estate representative) "hasn't heard from the attorney" and they "don't know where they are in the process". I have even heard from estate representatives themselves making similar comments.

One way to make sure you don't end up in this situation with your client is to lay out a sort of map of the process. This is especially true if you are an investor buying the property from the estate with no other agents involved. A great high level "map" of the process would be to lay out the three phases of probate.

The first phase is the appointment phase. This is where the probate case is filed with the court and they appoint either an executor or administrator. During this phase a will is produced if there is one or by matters of law they figure out who is going to be the executor or the administrator of the estate. This usually happens in months one and two. The appointment is complete when the court issues letters testamentary or letters of administration. Those letters are going to be needed by the title company for closing a transaction because they tell what powers the executor or administrator possesses. It's kind of like a driver's license. You don't drive until you have your license...same thing here, you don't sign contracts, you don't move forward in the process until you get those letters testamentary or letter of administration.

The next phase of the probate case is called the administration phase, this is the phase where the administrator/executor is going to search for all debts, seek out and notify creditors, seek out debtors, seek out all the assets of the estate, check for the validity of debts, etc. They may have to liquidate some assets in the estate in order to pay some debts, or produce liquidity. They are going to resolve the debtor issues and claims on the estate as well as resolve inheritance issues. Depending on the complexity of the probate case, issues with the heirs, quantity and types of assets and debts, this could be a long process (as I'm sure you can imagine). Typically it is months 2 through 8 in an average probate case.

The last phase is the closing phase and this is the phase in which executor or administrator gives the final report to the court. They will give an accounting to the court and to the beneficiaries. Additionally this is the phase where they actually distribute some of the assets or the remaining assets in estate to the beneficiaries based on the will or based on the law. The last thing they do is close the case. This typically occurs in months 9 through 12 on a typical one year probate. Now every probate case does not last a year but that is a good average. The beautiful thing about many probate sales is that they occur well within that year; usually during the administration phase.

This diagram will help you with a visual of the process:

PHASE 1 - APPOINTMENT	GENERAL TIME FRAME
• **Probate case is filed** • **Deceased person's Will (if any) is admitted to probate** • **Court appoints an estate representative (called either "Administrator" or "Executor")**	**Days 1 - 60**
PHASE 2 – ADMINISTRATION	
The Estate Representative: • Searches for deceased person's assets and debts • Obtains appraisal of all assets • Confirms validity of all debts • Liquidates (sells) some or all assets to pay valid debts • Resolves all claims and debts against estate • Resolves inheritance issues, if any	**Months 2 – 8** **(or later, depending upon complexity of the case)**

PHASE 3 – Closing	
The Estate Representative: • **Prepares final report and accounting for submission to court and beneficiaries for approval** • **Distributes net estate to beneficiaries according to the Will, or the laws of the State of California if there is no Will** • **Closes the case**	**Months 9 – 12** **(or later, depending upon complexity of the case)**

Know the Probate Real Estate Sale Process

Being successful at almost anything starts with knowledge about what you are doing. Almost daily I talk with real estate agents that need help understanding some process that has to do with our business. Probate is no different.

The previous pages should have given you a pretty good idea of the probate process....but as mentioned in the preface, we are not trying to become attorneys. The goal is to close a real estate transaction as either an investor or real estate agent. Therefore, it is more important that we become familiar with the Probate Sale Process. Go to www.ProbateRealEstateSales101.com for an outstanding one page chart on the process.

Agent/Investor Tip!

The Top 5 Reasons to Do Probate Real Estate (besides the fact that it can make you rich!)

Almost daily I talk with agents that ask me how to obtain more business. I become concerned when I hear the same questions for the 500th time like:

"What is a good area to farm?"

"How can I get listings?"

"What should I do to market myself?"

"How can I stand out from the crowd with my marketing?"

"How do I get the homeowners to list with me?"

Well the answer is…..market yourself to a specific niche. Since I am a probate specialist, I know that probate is an outstanding niche that can generate consistent volumes of listings for years to come! Here are the top 5 reasons to be in probate real estate today:

#5—There are 76 million Baby Boomers (people born between 1946 and 1964). Baby boomers have driven the U.S. economy from the start of the baby boom! They are responsible for everything from the growth of companies like Gerber and Johnson & Johnson back in the mid-20th century, to the explosion of "muscle cars", the huge infusion of money into the stock market in the 1990s (as they saved for retirement), to the reason health care is such a hot topic nowadays! Well, starting in 2011, every day about 8,000 people turn 65. These folks will be downsizing their homes, purchasing second homes, and unfortunately as they age, they will be dying. Like the saying goes, "There

are only two certain things in life...Death and Taxes". Only one of those things can create a business niche for us!

#4—More than 1 in 4 Californians are Baby Boomers. A study from the California Department of Health Services indicated that 27% of Californians are baby boomers. It has been said that Baby Boomers control 67% of U.S. wealth. That wealth often includes a home. Again, they are the aging population, and the real estate sales of the future and today.

#3—From our research, in urban areas as many as 85% of homes owned by individuals would end up in probate courts if the owners died. That is a huge percentage! There are far too many homeowners who have not properly prepared an estate plan.

#2—80% of probate real estate is free and clear or has a large amount of equity. Would you like a few regular sales where the price was extremely flexible? Equity sales are at a premium today and draw lots of buyers really fast. They are there waiting for you.... you just have to be in the right game to go get them!

#1—Agents with a niche sell more real estate. The top 10% of all real estate agents have some niche in which they do business. There are many reasons for it...for example:

- A niche enables you to develop a more compelling sales message.

- People search for agents based on a certain niche. We know that most sellers and buyers start their search online. Many times they start by searching some niche (i.e. googling "probate agents" or "Cheviot Hills real estate" or "Long Beach homes with a pool").

- Having a niche allows you to focus on 1 area and become an expert over time. You will eventually be the "go to" guy or gal for that niche.

- Your niche will differentiate you from your competition.

- A niche will generate referrals for you. If you are known as the "Marina Condo-Guy" or "Downtown Debbie", people will send you referrals without you even knowing it. It happens to me all the time! People know that I am an expert in probate so they refer other agents that are looking for someone who knows probate or has questions about probate, trusts and estates.

The funniest part about the niche is that it will increase your business and your referrals outside the niche too!! Imagine that. It is a strange phenomenon, but it is true, so promote yourself as a probate agent and you will find yourself having more short sales, regular listings, distressed property listings, etc.

Chapter 2 Types of Sales of Real Property

Probate Confirmation vs. Non-Confirmation

In the real estate business, don't we all want the same thing...more closed transactions? Whether you are a brand new agent who just got in the business or you've been in the business forever, you probably agree we all want more transactions to close. Yet oddly enough, I find it a strange phenomenon that a lot of people shy away from probate sales; especially court confirmation probate sales. We are going to start with the pros and cons of court confirmation sales and non-court confirmation sales (standard sales). By getting a better understanding of these transactions it will make it easier to stomach the challenges that may present themselves!

Since 1993, I have heard it said over and over... *"I don't want to deal with that probate situation."* Or worse than that, *"I don't want to deal with that probate because it requires court confirmation"*.

This avoidance of dealing with a probate situation has caused more loss of capital, increased expenses, waste of money and reduced assets being passed to the beneficiaries than any other factor! When you dig into the details of probate real estate transactions I think you will find that it really isn't so bad. In today's market, many probate sales close significantly faster than other transactions!

Whether you are the personal representative of an estate, a real estate agent, buyer of property, investor, heir or beneficiary, it will help to have a little better understanding of the process.

Although probate property is often sold in open court (in a "confirmation hearing"), estate representatives may also elect to sell without a confirmation hearing. The decision to sell with or without confirmation is generally made by the estate representative in consultation with his/her lawyer. The decision is usually based upon the facts of the case, the power given to the estate representative, the attitudes of the beneficiaries, and the state of the sales market.

The Pros of a Court Confirmation Sale

One of the main benefits of a court confirmation sale is that everything is well documented and approved by the court. This limits a lot of the objections by the other beneficiaries or other heirs. A key point to keep in mind is that you are dealing with family issues and the death of a family member. There may be fighting or lack of trust among the heirs, desire for revenge from something that happened in the past or many other issues. A court confirmation sale can squash a lot of quarreling between the heirs. It is not uncommon to see a confirmation hearing on cases where it is not even required because the administrator wants to protect themselves from problems.

The second benefit is that agents can potentially earn more commission in a court confirmation sale due to the competitive bidding process. The listing agent may sell the property or may obtain an accepted offer of $150,000. Then at the court confirmation hearing it gets bid up to $200,000. The commission on the property should be based on the ultimate sales price (see Chapter 4 for details on agents protecting your commission).

The third advantage of the court confirmation sale is that you get competitive bidding. In theory, this will allow the estate to receive the highest possible price for the property.

The Pros of the Non-Confirmation Sale

The non-confirmation sale is basically just like a regular sale. There may be a couple extra bits of paperwork but it is very similar to a regular transaction so you and your clients save time.

Another benefit is that it is much easier to explain a non-confirmation sale to a buyer/seller because it is very similar to regular real estate transaction.

The Cons of the Court Confirmation Sale

One of the biggest drawbacks is there is a longer time frame. Typically it takes 3-5 weeks or so to get the confirmation hearing scheduled. After the hearing it can take up to another two weeks to obtain the court orders necessary to close the real estate transaction. Working with the referee's opinion of value can cause delays (especially if the referee's opinion is too high).

Another drawback is that the buyer must compete with other offers. The confirmation hearing is just like an auction. Even though an offer is accepted subject to the court confirmation, there may be competitive bidding at that hearing and the original buyer may not win the bid (see Chapter 4 for the details of the Court Confirmation Sale).

The third drawback is that this process can be difficult to explain to buyers and sellers. Some buyers don't understand that even though their initial offer is accepted, they can be overbid in court. This scares off many buyers and especially investors who don't want their deposit tied up while waiting for a confirmation hearing. It is for this reason that I said it is *in theory* that a confirmation hearing brings the highest price for the property. Since some people avoid court confirmation sales, especially in the case of investors, it actually may not bring the highest possible sales price.

The Cons of the Non-Confirmation Sale

The beneficiaries or heirs may be more likely to fight when there's no confirmation hearing because they may not trust each other. The heirs may believe that the personal representative of the estate is not selling the property for the highest possible price so they can receive some side kickback. It can bring up arguments and objections because people think they're not getting everything they deserve. For this reason, some estates that have the power to sell without court confirmation still use the court confirmation process.

There may be some cases where doing a non-confirmation sale may cause additional costs. This is not always the case but depending on the situation, it could happen (particularly if the PR has trouble obtaining a bond).

Finally, in some cases, it may be difficult for an estate representative to obtain full authority and therefore sell the property without court confirmation because they cannot obtain a bond. The court requires a bonding company to provide a bond to cover errors, mistakes, fraud, etc. committed by the estate representative that may damage or diminish the benefit to the heirs. This bonding company will have their own requirements to approve the estate representative. If the bonding company will not approve the estate representative they will not likely receive full authority and therefore will not be able to sell without court confirmation. Poor credit is sometimes a reason a bonding company will turn down an estate representative.

> *Note: Bonds and the bonding companies are not usually things we have to worry about as the real estate professionals. The bond and matters regarding the type of authority the estate representative will receive are attorney/estate representative/court issues...not Real Estate Professional issues.*

This is a high level overview of some of the pros and cons of court confirmation sales and non-confirmation sales. We will cover these in more detail in Chapters 3 and 4.

Agent/Investor Tip!!

Working with the Estate Representative

"A problem is your opportunity to do your best"....Duke Ellington

The estate Representative is dealing with a problem: the death of someone. This is your opportunity to really do the best for them. Put your best foot forward and really go to work for them.

7 Steps to a Smooth Transaction

My goal is to help you on your real estate transaction:

- **Close fast**
- **Close with a simple process**
- **Close without problems**
- **Net the most amount of money possible to the estate or your client**

If these sound like your objectives, keep on reading.

1. Establish rapport with the attorney.

You are the real estate professional. The attorney is looking for someone who can sell the property quickly, cooperate with the legal and other issues and close the transaction on time. Exhibit these skills and you are taking the first step.

2. Call your title representative right away for a free transaction review.

The title company is involved in reviewing and recording some of the legal documents that pertain to real property transfers by the estate. Your title representative can help you avoid the "mine fields" in your transaction. Be sure to work with someone who has ample experience in probate transactions.

3. Obtain a copy of the letters testamentary or letters of administration.

You wouldn't practice medicine until after you graduate medical school and pass the exams, would you? Likewise, you must have a signed copy of the letters issued by the judge prior to acting on behalf of the estate. Get a copy of this from the estate representative prior to signing contracts. Don't put the cart before the horse!

4. Review the process with the Estate Representative.

This is the person that will be acting on behalf of the estate. Gather as much information from them as possible. Often times they will provide you with much needed info. You want to make sure everyone is on the same page and keep communication lines open with the representative.

5. Consult with the attorney on the case.

Again, make sure everyone is on the same page. This is such an important step as the attorney can help guide you through the rough waters of the transaction. Additionally, the attorney may inform you of information that the estate representative can't or won't give you. You know the saying, "There are two sides to every story".

6. Ensure your escrow officer/closing agent knows probate.

The escrow officer often touches every single piece of paper in a real estate transaction. There are usually additional documents required as part of a probate transaction and it is important that your escrow officer is familiar with these documents, their disposition and the process.

7. Open your title order with a company/representative that specializes in probate.

If you have a foreign car you probably take it to a mechanic that works on foreign cars. If you have a heart problem, you probably go to a cardiac specialist rather than an orthopedic surgeon. Likewise, take your probate transaction to a title representative and company that specialize in probate.

I am sure that you want the sale of the house to go to escrow and close in a short time without any hang-ups. In today's market, that is not as easy as it once was! The key is to assemble a team of specialists that

cover all ends and prevent the glitches that sometimes come up.

Chapter 3 Full Authority Sale

Letters Testamentary/Letters of Administration

Let's start by defining these two documents, and then we will get to the meat of the subject!

The court issues letters testamentary when there is an executor. The court issues letters of administration when they appoint an administrator. An "executor" carries out the directions and requests set forth in the decedent's will. An "administrator" is appointed by the court to manage the estate of a decedent who dies intestate (with no will). Therefore, if there was a will, you will have an executor. If there was no will, there will be an administrator. Generally, for our real estate transactions it doesn't matter whether we are dealing with letters testamentary or letters of administration, executor or administrator. The person in that role basically performs the same functions. The term estate representative refers to either executor or administrator.

The letters are usually issued 30-60 days after the probate case is filed. The important thing to note on the court ordered letters is whether the estate representative is given full or limited authority. Full authority means that the estate representative can typically sell the property without court supervision. This type of sale would be almost exactly like a regular sale for those of us in real estate. Limited Authority means the court must supervise all the actions of the estate representative. A sale with limited authority is going to require court confirmation.

Before the court issues the court ordered letters, no one has authority to act on behalf of the estate. No one! It doesn't matter if they tell you they are the oldest son, the only child, the spouse, or anything. No one has the legal power to act on behalf of neither the decedent nor the estate until those letters have been issued. So it's kind of like driving before you have a driver's license.

Most people wouldn't think of driving without a license yet I have seen agents start real estate transactions before those letters are issued. I've had files where they had listed the property, signed disclosures, signed contracts, without ever getting the letters testamentary on the case. This is a mistake! I even had one file where they were a week away from closing the escrow without ever seeing the letters testamentary. We later learned that the letters hadn't been issued! Therefore they were ready to close, so they thought, but no one had the authority to act on behalf of the estate. The listing was invalid, the sales contract was invalid...the whole thing was invalid. Luckily, they were able to re-do everything and close the transaction about 3 months later.

The best thing to remember is to start at the beginning! Begin by obtaining a copy of the letters testamentary or letters of administration from the estate representative or from the attorney and know what you are working with. A plain copy is fine in the beginning, but a certified copy is required at the time of closing the transaction.

The Full Authority Sale

A full authority sale is almost the same as a regular sale. Of course you are going to use the probate listing agreement, the probate contract, etc. That just makes logical sense. But the process is not much different. It is important to note that probate listings are supposed to be 90 day listings. You will notice on the California Association of Realtors contracts that 90 days is specified as the period for the listing agreement.

When you put the property on the MLS, you will also specify that it is a probate sale. It is to your advantage to indicate that the sale does not require court confirmation. That helps open the market to more buyers as many do not want to go through the overbid process of a court confirmation sale. Once the property is on the MLS you market the property as normal until you receive an acceptable offer.

Once you have an acceptable offer that your seller (the executor/administrator) accepts, it is important to let the attorney know as soon as possible. The attorney will prepare and file a notice of proposed action with the court. This notice informs all interested parties in the estate that the property is being sold and for what amount. The attorney also mails the notice to the interested parties. Those parties have 15 days to object to the sale. The attorney deals with this process, but it is important for you as the agent to know what is going on in the background.

Prior to closing your transaction, the title insurance company is going to need to see a copy of the notice of proposed action. The majority of the time, the attorney just emails a copy of it over along with verification that there are no objections to the sale or that all objections have been resolved. The 15 day period from the filing of the notice of proposed action must pass prior to closing the sale of the property. In cases where there is a very short escrow or for other reasons, the parties to the case can waive their right to notice. There is a specific form filed in such cases.

Once the time period has passed or the waivers have been obtained, the transaction can be closed. There is one other thing that the title insurance company is going to require. The presence of a lien for state or federal estate taxes against the estate would actually become a lien secured against the real estate. Therefore, prior to closing, the title company will want verification that there are no state or federal estate taxes due. This usually comes in the form of a one sentence email from the attorney that "there are no estate taxes due". If however there are estate taxes due, the title company would pay those taxes out of the proceeds of the sale. The dollar amount of those taxes would be provided to the title company in order to pay such taxes.

Review

With these simple items that are handled by the attorney, your full authority probate sale is ready to close! To make sure this comes through clear and simple, let me itemize the additional items needed on a full authority sale as opposed to a standard sale from a living seller:

1. The title company needs a certified copy of the letters testamentary/letters of administration indicating full authority has been given to the executor/administrator.

2. The title company will require a copy of the notice of proposed action filed with the court, verifying that the 15 day objection time period has passed or been waived by all parties. A note from the attorney indicating that there are no objections to the sale.

3. A note from the attorney that there are no estate taxes due (or provide the amounts due so that they can be paid).

Chapter 4 Court Confirmation Sale

There are a lot of myths about court confirmation sales and the steps involved. Let's walk through this step by step.

- First, the probate case is filed with the court just like in all probate cases.

- Usually somewhere around 30-60 days later, the judge will issue letters testamentary or letters of administration. Those letters will declare who is in charge of the estate and whether they have full or limited authority. Court confirmation is required when there is limited authority. At times, for the protection of the estate representative, beneficiaries or other reasons, there may be a court confirmation sale even though the representative has full authority. There are also situations where a trustee of a trust who normally does not require any probate proceedings at all, will utilize a court confirmation sale. When there is a sale coming out of a conservatorship or guardianship, there will often be a court ordered sale. Again, a court confirmation sale is usually done for the protection of the trustee, executor, administrator and/or heirs, beneficiaries, the child (guardianship), or the conservatee.

- Once letters are issued, the estate representative has the authority to act on behalf of the estate. Depending on what other issues there are in the estate, it may be time to list the property. Consult the attorney for direction as to when it is time to sell.

- A court referee will be appointed by the court to give an opinion of value of the property. Note that I wrote "opinion of value". The referee probably does not go to the property and certainly does not do an interior inspection so I find it very hard to call it an appraisal. They are required to take a photo of the property (usually from the street), but they won't usually know anything about the property other than what the photo tells them. They just come up with a value based on comparable sales. The property needs to sell for 90% of the referee's opinion of value. Therefore, when dealing with a property that is a fixer or in bad condition, take note of the condition of the property. Are there any factors that limit the marketability of the property? Is the immediate street/neighborhood a detriment to the price? What repairs are necessary? Take photos. Obtain contractors' estimates. Write a summary. Do a BPO (broker's price opinion). All this information could become very useful and you may want to make the court referee aware of these factors (you would do that by providing the information to the attorney for the estate to give to the referee). Remember you are the real estate professional and it may be necessary to inform the referee of what the actual market value of the property is since you are the "feet on the ground". It is more difficult to *change* the referee's opinion of value once it has been given than it is to educate them up front. By doing a great job of communicating to the attorney the details of the property, you can be a great help to the estate. Most people who are not real estate professionals are going to look up the property on Zillow or a similar site. If they are savvier, they may have information from the MLS (Multiple Listing Service) through an agent, or info from a title company.

However, none of these sources tell us about the good or bad things about a neighborhood, like vandalism and crime, landscape views, proximity to negative influences, or other non-statistical information that affects the value of real property. As a real estate agent or investor, you can be the professional to provide this information. As a result, you will be an asset to the attorney and the estate.

- The agent will list and market the property. The agent will receive offers on the property and again, the accepted offer should be 90% of the court referee's opinion of value.

- With accepted offer in hand, the attorney will request the court date for the confirmation hearing. At the time of writing this book, it takes about 3-4 weeks to obtain the court confirmation hearing date in Los Angeles County. While the attorney is getting the court date the real estate agent will keep marketing the property and let people see the property. The agent should let other potential buyers do their due diligence. They may want to pay for an appraisal, do a home inspection, termite inspection or whatever due diligence they need to do. The real estate agent should allow them to do this due diligence and continue to market the property. The agent should also promote the upcoming hearing so everyone knows about the court confirmation sale. The more bidders present at the confirmation hearing, the more benefit to the estate.

- The confirmation hearing is like an auction. The judge says "The property up now is 123 Main St. The accepted offer is $xx.xx. Who is going to overbid? The next overbid is $xxx.xx." From there the bidding starts. Prior to the bidding the attorney will look over the proof of funds and deposit checks of all the bidders. The bidders (buyers) need to have cashier's checks for 10% of the price they are willing to pay for the property. Most of the time the check will be payable to the escrow company they are going to use, but sometimes they want it payable to the law firm or the estate. Consult the listing agent or attorney for guidance here. The bidders also need to have proof of funds or a loan approval letter to show they can complete the sale.

- Usually the first overbid will be 5% plus $500 higher than the accepted offer. From there the bidding usually goes in $1,000 increments. Again, this confirmation hearing is like an auction. Once they reach a final price, the judge will bring down the gavel and say the property is sold for that value.

- The successful bidder needs to know a couple of things: First, it is a no contingency sale. Therefore, their offer is not subject to appraisal; it's not subject to lender approval nor termite nor other inspections. The due diligence on the property should be done before the hearing so that they are ready to close after the hearing. The buyer will have time to process their loan during the regular escrow period, but does not have contractual contingencies. Second, the escrow will be opened usually the day after the court confirmation hearing.

- Roughly about one-two weeks after the confirmation hearing the court order that was drafted by the attorney will be signed by the judge. Once the court order is approved and signed escrow is ready to close. However, it is normal to see a 30 day escrow period after the confirmation hearing. It is a good idea to review this order prior to it being submitted to the court for the judge's signature. There are sometimes mistakes made and it is better to catch those mistakes up front rather than after the judge has signed the order.

Important Note:

We must note that several of the details covered in this chapter are subject to local procedural differences. As mentioned in the disclaimer, the Probate Code is the same throughout any given state, but it is common to see procedural differences in different regions. For example, in San Bernardino County, the courts are pretty strict about needing a deposit on a probate sale of 10% of the sales price. However, in Los Angeles County it is not uncommon to see a deposit of 5%. It is important to know these procedural differences for your area. Usually you can go on the website of the court that governs your region and read the procedures on their site.

Agents, Protect Your Commission

- The guideline for listing percentage is 5%. When there are extenuating circumstances, you can petition the court to have the listing be more than that. For instance, most vacant land listings are 10%. If the probate listing is not 10%, it will not be as competitive on the market and therefore may not command the same price.
- Put commission specifics on the MLS, on the listing agreement and everywhere possible so that it is clear. Here is one way I have seen it written on a typical 5% listing: Commission to

be split only with the agent of the successful bidder, <u>2.5% to selling agent, 2.5% to listing agent based on the final sales price</u>. There are variations of the exact words you use, so check with your broker for specifics. Listing Agents: make sure that your commission is based on the final sales price, that way no one can cut you out on the difference between your accepted offer and the final sales price.

- Have the attorney put commission specifics on court order. It is normal to see commission written on line 12 of the court order like this: *...in the amount of:* $12,500 (5% of the sales price) *to be paid as follows (specify):* $6,250 to ABC Realty who represented the seller and $6,250 to XYZ Realty who represented the successful over bidder. ($250,000 sale price x .05). Again, this will lock it in so there are no disputes over what you are supposed to be paid as the listing agent.
- Investors who are planning to bid should bring an agent with them. You should be represented by *someone*. If you don't have an agent, the listing agent will be happy to represent you. But why not create a relationship with an agent of your choosing. One that can bring you more business...think of an agent that you want a referral relationship with...maybe it *is* the listing agent. Whoever you choose, just be deliberate and strategic. It could be a great way to develop a relationship with the listing agent.

FHA and VA Buyers Can Buy a Probate Property

A lot of people think if they have a VA or FHA buyer they cannot buy the property at a court confirmation sale. Heck, it's easy to see why…we just wrote that on a court confirmation sale they want a 10% deposit check. Read this excerpt from an interview with an agent:

Samantha: That entirely is not true. This person that came to me loved the home, but he was a veteran. He had no money, but he had excellent credit. So what we did was we had a VA lender submit to the Veterans Affairs for his certificate that showed that yes, he indeed, did serve the armed forces, and it was a no down, no closing cost loan, and it's just like a regular sale. The only thing we did different was we had all the inspections and everything completed before we went to the Court Confirmation.

Kevin: Right, I think that's a very big point to make because on Court Confirmation the buyer can be in jeopardy of losing whatever deposit they have in escrow, and kind of need to close at that point. It's good they did all the inspections up front.

Samantha: Exactly, we do everything up front before Court Confirmation. That's actually the last step, before Court Confirmation.

Kevin: Right, that's good. So on that VA purchase, since it was a no-money down loan, did they have to put a deposit in escrow on that transaction?

Samantha: You know, he actually did, and he didn't have a lot of money, so the owners allowed him to put 500 dollars down, which for the buyer, that was a lot of money. He really didn't have a whole lot of money, but he had such wonderful credit and they understood. So, we put that in and at the close of escrow the money came back to him.

Kevin: And, what a wonderful way to close a transaction. Help the estate out and also help out a veteran. What a wonderful way to give back to our country, so that sounds great.

It is important to note that the Court Confirmation sales are "no contingency" sales. So have all your due diligence done up front. Also, as an agent or investor, we must know that the court is going to do what is in the best interest of the estate. If the best interest of the estate is to open the sale up to the pool of veterans that may be interested and/or FHA buyers that may be interested, the courts will likely oblige. After all, the larger the pool of buyers, the more demand there is for the home and the higher the price for the property. You just have to make the case to the attorney/courts that it is in the best interest of the estate to accept such an offer with a modified down payment.

Agent/Investor Tip!

I have seen sales stopped or delayed months because of an incorrect "opinion of value" from the court referee. I cannot stress enough the fact that agents/investors need to address this opinion of value up front. It is a major issue if the property is worth $200,000 or that is the amount you want to purchase it for but the referee's opinion of value is filed at $300,000. Remember, in court confirmation sales the judge will likely reject any sale that is not 90% of that opinion of value.

I am actually in the middle of a transaction right now where the referee indicated the property was worth $450,000. The property was actually listed on the market for 8 months for that amount, however it didn't sell. In our hot Southern California market, houses are not sitting unsold for 8 months. When we opened escrow the agent indicated that the referee was going to change the value of their "appraisal". Even though we had repeated discussions about this, the agent continued to assure me that the "opinion of value" issue was already addressed by him with the attorney and/or referee and that it was going to be changed. You see, the property will not sell for anything more than about $340,000.

Many investors had lost interest in this property and did not want to make offers because they did not want their money held up in the court process for a few months. The attorney on this case would not even request a court date until an offer was accepted and a $40,000 deposit was paid. There would be about a month to wait for the court hearing after that and then the escrow period if that investor was the winning bidder. In our market currently, investors don't want their cash tied up for that long.

Finally, it came time for the court confirmation hearing. The offer of about $340,000 was the winning bid. Everything was going to be fine and we are going to open a 10 day escrow, right? Wrong! The judge rejected the offer because it was not within 90% of the referee's opinion of value. Now, the fastest way for the heirs to sell the property and obtain the proceeds is to distribute the property to them and have them sell as individuals. This will take a few more months and let's hope there are no other issues that present themselves.

The key learning here is that the referee's opinion of value will not take into account: market conditions specific to a particular property, the state of mind of investors who are the only buyers for a particular property, all the repairs necessary to sell a property at fair market value, issues in the local neighborhood that limit a property's value, substandard conditions, abatements on a property, etc...unless a professional brings it to their attention. Be that professional.

Agent/Investor Tip!

I inherited a property, do I need title insurance?

If you've just inherited a piece of property or are buying it from your family's estate, you may need title insurance. What is title insurance? It's actually very different from the insurance we normally buy for our home or car. Whether you inherited the real estate through probate by going through probate court or through a revocable living trust, there are issues that could arise with the property that title insurance will protect you from.

Even if the home has been in your family for years, or even generations, someone other than your family or the person you think of as the owner of the property could own mineral, air or utility rights to the property. The city could even have an easement giving it the right to string utility lines across the front yard. There could also be liens on your property that you'll want to know about.

Liens on the property could be held by a bank with a mortgage, someone who has done work on the house and filed a lien against it, federal, state or local governments or creditors just to name a few. Dealing with all of this could be even worse than going through probate and if you already had to go through probate court to get the house in the first place, this is a hassle you don't need.

The first thing a title company will do is perform a title search. A title search will reveal many of these potential problems and is done simply by examining public records to look up the history of property ownership. The title search shows not only limitations on the use of the property and rights others may have to it, but also liens or monetary obligations that are outstanding against the property.

Title insurance covers events relating to the title that have already happened. It does not cover anything that happens after the date of issuance. For example if you inherited a house from your grandmother and she had a lien put on it for taxes she didn't pay in the past, title insurance would be a great asset. If, on the other hand, you got the house and failed to pay taxes for five years, title insurance wouldn't help in this situation.

To protect yourself, you can look into getting title insurance before you actually take the property in your name. Before offering to issue a title insurance policy, an insurance company will do a title search to find out whether there are any problems or limitations with the title. This search is done in an effort to reduce the company's risk. This helps in two ways. First, by minimizing the risks of claims being made, title insurance companies can offer insurance for a fairly low, one-time fee. Second, problems with deeds, wills and trusts that contain improper vesting, incorrect names, outstanding mortgages, judgments, tax liens or other problems are typically found through the title search and usually can be cleared up before you inherit the property or go through probate.

A good title company can help you uncover potential issues with the property so it is a good idea to get them involved early. Every circumstance is different so it is important to listen to the advice of your attorney. They will provide information to you on how best to proceed in order to protect your asset.

Chapter 5 Fast Probates! (Avoiding "Full" Probate)

Spousal Order

Have you ever talked with a person about listing their home only to find out later that the property is in the deceased spouse's name? This dilemma has crossed my desk countless times. Sometimes the surviving spouse doesn't even know that their name was not on title. The surviving spouse may have been removed from title during a mortgage transaction, because they had pending liens, or for a myriad of other reasons. Whatever the reason, it is nice to know that there may be a fast way to resolve this issue so the surviving spouse may claim the ownership of the property.

First and foremost, let me address that when I mention a spouse that also includes a domestic partner or registered domestic partner. The court forms in many jurisdictions indicate spouse or domestic partner right on the form. Check with your jurisdiction to be sure, but throughout this book, these words are interchangeable.

A spousal petition asks that the decedent's property pass to the surviving spouse without full probate administration. I could explain that community property can be passed this way but separate property is only passed this way if there is a will with the spouse as the sole beneficiary. I could explain what happens if the will provides several beneficiaries and what happens if there is no will. I could explain that a person receiving property this way may be responsible for the decedent's debts. There are probably a million other minute details we could discuss here, but we are not trying to become attorneys and I would probably get some of it wrong! We are trying to close a real estate transaction and do it the best way possible.

The key thing to remember is that there is potentially a way to pass property to the surviving spouse without the time and expense of full probate administration. These petitions often are signed by the judge with no actual hearing. A hearing is not required unless the petition is objected to or someone requests the hearing. It is common to see properly filed petitions with all procedures followed simply approved by the courts.

How long does it take?

The time period is relatively short. An attorney that I have worked with for over 15 years indicated she can complete these petitions and affidavits in 90 days or less. Obviously every case is different, but I have seen a pretty fast turnaround on these petitions allowing my clients (real estate agents) to close their transactions. Seek a good attorney to help with these matters and help the surviving spouse save time, money and headaches.

Heggstad Order

Have you ever seen a property in which the deceased owner had a trust but never put this property in the trust? What about the scenario where the decedent put the property in the trust but took it out as required by a lender to refinance the mortgage? At the death of the owner if the property is not in the trust, as we have already established, the property must go through probate in order to pass title to the heirs or sell the property. Well, in the situation where the owner had a trust but did not hold the property in that trust, there may be hope for avoiding a full probate case!

Case law in California has provided a solution to this problem without going through full probate administration. Through an abbreviated proceeding, the court can order that the property which was not held in the trust *IS IN FACT* held in the trust. This is a relatively simple procedure but there are some requirements that must be met. For instance, it has to be proven that the asset was intended to be held in the trust. The procedure for obtaining this order from the court is commonly called a "Heggstad Petition" for the 1993 California case Estate of Heggstad, 16 CA4th 943, 20 CR2d 433.

Heggstad petitions are quite common and there are numerous transactions that I have closed using court orders that came from Heggstad petitions. It is important to work with a good attorney on these situations.

How long does it take?

The time period is relatively short...I have heard attorneys quote as little as 30-45 days to my clients seeking such a petition. Obviously every case is different, but I have seen a fast turnaround on these petitions allowing my clients (real estate agents) to close their transactions. An agent trying to close a real estate sale is usually quite happy to hear this news! The heirs, beneficiaries, and successor trustees of the trust are usually quite happy too!

Small Probates

Did you know that there is still another way to pass an interest in a property to the heirs without doing a full blown probate?

I'm talking about the portion of the probate code called Section 13000-14000. It's a portion that deals with small estates and the part that typically is used to pass real property through to heirs in estates under $150,000.00. Small probate administration can be handled in a few different ways. In California, estates are considered small if they are worth $150,000 or less. These small estates can be settled without formal probate proceedings by using a relatively simple petition procedure. This summary form of probate is available whether the assets are real property or personal property. According to probate laws there are, however, specific requirements that must be met. See an attorney for details.

Now I know here in sunny Southern California (and many other areas throughout the country) we don't often find estates that are under $150,000.00 if there is real estate involved. However, you may be dealing with a partial interest. For instance, recently I worked on a transaction where there were four parties on title to the property. The deceased party had a quarter interest in the property. That quarter interest and the rest of the items in their estate were worth less than a

$150,000.00. According to the attorney, this section of the probate code applied and they closed their real estate transaction without a long probate case.

Today, right before writing this portion of this book I was talking with an agent about a situation on a vacant piece of land up in the high desert where properties sell for much lower dollar amounts. Two of the tenants-in-common are deceased and the other two did not want any expensive long drawn out process to sell the property. If there would in fact be a long process, the two remaining tenants-in-common did not want to proceed with the sale. It appears this code section will apply in this case. It will be very inexpensive to resolve and will only take 6-8 weeks or so. I told him to see a good probate attorney!

There is even more good news for those small estates and small interest in real property. If the interest in the real property (the decedent's interest) is worth less than $50,000 on the date of death, the successor to that interest can transfer it with an affidavit procedure rather than the petition procedure. Essentially, an affidavit is drawn up with the proper verbiage and that document is used to transfer the property to the successor to that property. To be sure that this is done correctly it is still advisable to obtain legal counsel, however this is a far less costly and less time consuming procedure than even the petition procedure. You can even find copies of the petitions for many counties online. You gotta love Google! Now we just have to hope that when we find a property with a deceased party that the decedent's interest is worth less than $50,000!

NOTE:

> There are some contrary views from legal professionals that I have heard or read that indicate one cannot transfer real property via an

affidavit of small estate. However, as my examples previously discussed as well as several other transactions that I have closed have indicated...it can be done. My hunch is that the details make all the difference and that different attorneys interpret the law differently. It is so important with all these matters to make sure you work with an attorney that is very experienced in various types of probate matters.

How long does this process take?

If the case satisfies the requirements for small probate administration, the parties can settle your case without a long and expensive trip to probate court. Probate administration for small estates will not only save time and money, it will save stress and help the heirs complete getting the assets more quickly and easily than going through the full probate process.

Anyone who is entitled to inherit property from the deceased can settle the estate and get the title or possession of the property with these probate transfer procedures. In most cases, everything can be completed a few weeks after the required 40-day waiting period (or in some circumstances there can be a six-month waiting period). Depending on the exact circumstances, there may also be some filings and/or hearings that must be done with the court.

Now, Probate Code Section 13000 has a lot of intricate details and there is way more to it than most of us even care to know. However, it is important to remember that it exists because it may apply in certain circumstances. As always, consult a good attorney. A full blown probate case may take 8 months to a year, or more to finalize the estate. Whereas, this limited short term or an abbreviated probate, as it is often called can take 60 to 90 days or even less.

Full Authority

Chapter 3 outlines the details of full authority sales. I thought it was worth mentioning here that a full authority, non-court confirmation sale can be quite quick. As mentioned in Chapter 3 it is very similar to a regular sale. On numerous occasions, I have been told by attorneys that the property would be ready to be listed/sold within 6-8 weeks. This is on properties where the probate hadn't even been filed yet. Therefore, full authority sales are quite often fast sales even though the probate process may continue on for months or even years after the sale of the property.

Do I Need An Attorney For Probate?

An agent referred their client to me so I ended up speaking with the estate representative. The estate representative filed the probate case by herself and after a short time she realized she was in over her head. She quickly found out that there was more to representing herself in court than she originally thought. I commended her for realizing this so soon and I referred her to a great attorney. I am sure they lived happily ever after.

People often ask, "do I need an attorney to do my probate?" The answer is "no", almost anything you do in court can be done yourself. But if you were a brain surgeon and you had a brain tumor, would you do the surgery on yourself?

I spoke to a genius one time, who was very adamant about doing his probate himself. Now as the title rep doing his transaction, it doesn't make any difference to me. Really the only difference for us in the real estate business is that if they don't have an attorney they might not be doing things right and that can cause problems, delays, lawsuits, etc.

But I couldn't bear to let this genius go without helping him. Yet he knew so strongly that he didn't need an attorney, that any convincing I tried to do would be perceived as an argument. So I said "Let me ask you a question. At what point do you file the notice of proposed action and what is the waiting period after you file that notice?" To which he replied "The notice of what?" I said "That's exactly my point. You don't know what you're supposed to do, when you're supposed to do it, neither the timeframes nor the legalities of any of your actions. By not knowing you could jeopardize everything that you're doing. You could jeopardize the sale transaction that you're working on and subject yourself to personal liability."

In the end, I think he got it and hired an attorney. The point is that if you don't know everything that you are doing, if you haven't read all the laws, and if you haven't been trained on how to do it properly- you're better off getting an attorney! It's worth the money. Pay for it and make everything go smoothly and live happily ever after.

"He who represents himself in court has a fool for a client."

Confucius

So why do people want to avoid an attorney?

The most frequent reason I have seen is to avoid paying the attorney's fees. Have you heard the phrase "stepping over dollars to pick up pennies"? For most people it is a lack of understanding of how probate works. It can also be that some people have been scared by the attorneys that are sharks (we have all heard horror stories, and believe me I have been around plenty). But it is important to obtain a better understanding here.

Maximum probate fees are regulated by the probate code. The attorney cannot actually collect their fees until it is ordered by the judge. This usually happens at the closing of the estate when all of the final accounting is being done...after the sale of the property. The attorney may ask for a retainer or some money to cover out of pocket court costs and other expenses, but cannot actually collect their attorney's fees until after the judge has approved and ordered those fees paid (see chapter 9, How Much Does Probate Cost?).

It doesn't make sense for someone to avoid transferring property worth hundreds of thousands of dollars because of the attorney's fees. Once the property has been transferred out of the estate the new owners can obtain a loan to pay the attorney's fees if they are keeping the property. In the case of a sale, the proceeds generated from the sale can be used to pay the attorney's fees. If you were offered $300,000 cash, but at the time of receiving the money you had to pay a $10,000 fee to someone, wouldn't that be worth it? (Note: I said you pay the $10,000 fee at the time of receiving your money...this is not an email scam from some foreign government!! LOL)

Agent/Investor Tip!

Whenever possible, work with an attorney! If your client wants to do the probate without one, have one on standby. Can you imagine someone working on a Heggstad order or using any of the small probate administration laws that was not an attorney? It is just a formula for disaster! As an investor or agent, it is nice to let the professionals in law do their part so we can do our part.

Chapter 6 Avoiding Probate Altogether

Let's make sure we have a proper understanding here. This book is about probate sales of real property. I am a probate specialist and work with probate transactions daily, but probate court proceedings can be long, expensive and frustrating. I provide a lot of services to help people through the process of a selling, refinancing or transferring real property that goes through probate. However, probate is a costly process that for most situations is nothing more than a waste of money and the decedent's assets due to lack of preparation. The smart move is to avoid probate altogether!

Maybe this chapter will help in your personal situation. Maybe it will help you find properties that you thought were going to be in probate court, but do not have to go through that process. As an agent or investor that is active in probate real estate, at some point, you will come across situations and information discussed in this chapter.

There are several ways to avoid probate in California. How one holds title to their property makes all the difference. It is a good idea for homeowners to obtain legal advice before deciding how to hold title to their property.

Transfer-On-Death Deeds

Some states have established transfer-on-death (TOD) deeds or "beneficiary deeds". These are basically deeds that state who the property will pass to upon the death of the owner. Think of it like a bank account on which you indicate a beneficiary. This type of deed allows the property to pass to another individual without going through the probate procedure. See the list of states that allow TOD deeds below:

District of Columbia	Hawaii	Illinois
Indiana	Kansas	Minnesota
Missouri	Montana	Nebraska
Nevada	New Mexico	North Dakota
Ohio	Oklahoma	Oregon
South Dakota	Virginia	Washington
Wisconsin	Wyoming	*California

*California has recently passed a law to create the revocable transfer on death deed. This deed will be effective as of January 1, 2016. At the time of updating this material, all the details about these deeds are not yet clear and copies of the deed format have not been reviewed by the author. This is a major change in what is available to California property owners to pass properties to their heirs. Details will be available and updated at www.ProbateRealEstateSales101.com.

If this law stays in effect (there is a sunset period on this law in 2021) and becomes widely used, it may dramatically reduce the amount of probate transactions that take place. However, agents and investors should not worry about lack of transactions. This will probably not decrease the amount of transactions (listings or investment opportunities) available. It will only limit the number of transactions that actually have to go through probate first. The use of this new "TOD" deed will make it easier to complete the transactions as there will be no court matter involved.

In a nutshell, the determining factor on whether there is a sale or not never had anything to do with whether there was a probate case or not. It was the death of the owner that triggered the sale. The heirs either determined that they did not want the property or could not keep the property. The death of the owner is what triggered the sale...not the fact that there is a probate case.

Becoming an expert or a specialist in probate will generate more transactions for the agent or investor whether this deed is widely used or not. Essentially, being a specialist in "probate" generates trust sales, probate sales, "TOD deed" sales and all transactions where there has been a death of the owner. The average consumer does not differentiate between the different types of transactions. Therefore, your probate marketing will generate calls that end up being trust sales, TOD deed sales and other transactions where there is a deceased owner.

Joint Tenancy

Two or more people holding title to a property can specify that they hold title as joint tenants (for joint tenancy, you *MUST* specify that is how you are holding title...it is not presumed). In this type of ownership, when one person dies, the property is 100% owned by the remaining joint tenants. This ownership vesting on title to a property supersedes any trust or will that the person may have.

Joint tenancy is not the recommended way to pass assets that may increase in value to the heirs in many cases. The surviving joint tenant will not receive a "stepped-up cost basis" to fair market value at the date of death of the other joint tenant.

Holding Property in an Entity

Holding property in a legal entity such as a corporation, partnership, or LLC is another way of avoiding the probate courts. However, these entities come with enough other considerations to write another book! There are taxes to be paid, annual filings that have to be done, paperwork, bookkeeping, etc. This is not to mention that succession or estate planning still must be in place when the owner of the entity dies.

Trusts

One of the best ways to avoid all the hassle and headache that comes with probate court is to set up a trust for your estate. Setting up a trust is a great way to keep you and your family clear of probate court and preserve more of your assets for your heirs. Having your assets passed to your heirs through probate is often a huge waste of your and your heirs' resources. Isn't it better to plan ahead!

One of the most common trusts used is a living trust. In fact, in California you can make a living trust to avoid probate for virtually anything you own, including real estate, bank accounts, vehicles and more. To set up a living trust you need to create a trust document that names someone to take over as trustee after your death. This person is called a successor trustee. (See glossary for more definitions of terms)

Once you have set up the successor trustee, you must transfer ownership of your property to yourself as the trustee of the trust (or whoever is designated as trustee of the trust). After that the property will be controlled by the terms of the trust. When you do pass on, your successor trustee will generally be able to transfer your property to the trust beneficiaries without probate court proceedings.

Why is a Trust Better Than a Will?

Well, I have personal experience on this question. My grandfather set up a will because it was "cheaper" than setting up a trust. When he passed away, it cost my father and his siblings thousands of dollars to pass my grandfather's estate on to themselves. Had he spent the extra few dollars to set up a trust instead, it would have cost them $0 to take possession of the assets. My father always says "If you own a house, you should have a trust".

It is extremely important that you consult professional advice when considering what the best estate plan is for you and your loved ones. You should take a comprehensive look at all factors pertaining to the estate and the plan before making decisions as there may be some circumstances in which a will is the best choice.

What is a Living Trust?

In layman's terms, a living trust is simply directions for your estate you create while you're alive, rather than directions that are created at your death under the terms of your will or the probate code. Far too many people let the California Probate Code dictate what is going to happen to their assets when they pass on. Why not take control of that process and protect what you have worked so hard for!

Creating a trust is similar to creating a corporation. You set up an entity that has the legal control over your estate, or whichever assets you choose. The living trust exists only on paper, but it is capable of controlling property. You can be the trustee of your own living trust and maintain control over all the property until the time of your death.

Living trusts are designed to avoid probate. Some also help you save on death taxes and others let you set up long-term property management.

Living trusts help you avoid probate because the property you transfer into a living trust before your death doesn't go through probate at all. In a living trust the successor trustee simply transfers ownership of your real property and assets to the beneficiaries you named in the trust upon your death. In many cases, the whole process takes only a few weeks and best of all there are no attorney or court fees to pay. Once your property has been transferred to the beneficiaries the living trust is dissolved.

Fund the Trust

Now we have established that if you want your loved ones to avoid the pain of going through probate and probate court, you need to have a living trust. What do you look for in a trust, specifically a living trust or a revocable living trust? For a living trust to work properly, you have to transfer your assets into it. Title for your real estate and assets must be changed from your name to the name of the trustees of your trust, so that they will be held within the trust. Because your name is no longer on the title as an individual (instead you are on title as a trustee), there is no reason for the court to get involved if you become incapacitated or if you pass away. This makes it very easy for your successor trustee to step in and manage your financial affairs and avoid dealing with probate court.

This is done through a deed to the trustees of the trust. Without this deed to the trustees of the trust, constructive notice is not given to the world that the property is held under the trust. In other words, without the deed there would have to be a court proceeding in order to use the trust to avoid a regular probate proceeding. Case law has provided for this type of abbreviated proceeding in some circumstances and is known as a Heggstad order (see chapter 5).

Let's Define the Parties Involved in a Trust:

This is not meant to be an all-encompassing definition of a trust. You just want to know enough info so that when you are dealing with trusts that you will know the parties involved.

First, there is the grantor. Also called settler, trustor, creator or trust maker, the grantor is the person who sets up the trust. If you are the one putting the real estate or other property in the trust, you are the grantor. If you and your spouse set up a single trust together you are co-grantors of the trust. Typically, only the grantor or grantors can make changes to the trust.

Then there is the trustee. The trustee manages the assets in the trust. With real estate, the trustees names are actually on title to the property (see example below). Many people choose to be their own trustee and continue to manage their affairs for as long as they can.

John Doe as trustee of the John Doe family living trust dated 12-1-2001

A successor trustee is the person chosen to manage the living trust when the trustee is no longer able to handle the responsibilities. This usually happens when the grantor (who can also be the trustee) passes away or becomes incapacitated. Most living trusts will name multiple successor trustees in case one or more of the original choices die or becomes incapacitated or chooses not to serve as successor trustee. Sometimes two or more individuals are named to act together and other times a corporate trustee, like a bank or fiduciary company is chosen. It can also be a combination of the two.

The beneficiaries are the people or organizations who will receive the real estate and/or other trust assets after the grantor dies. Whether it is children, grandchildren, a favorite charity or anyone else, the beneficiaries are the receivers of the assets.

These four parties make up the living trust system. It is important that you pick people or entities that are best suited to handle their particular role in the living trust. To make sure that the beneficiaries can avoid probate you also need to know who the trustees are, who the successor trustees are, the order in which they receive powers and if they will be acting alone or with someone else.

With real estate transactions, knowing the parties involved is an important part of dealing with a trust. Your escrow and title company will need to know up front who the parties are that will be involved in the transaction. Often the first questions escrow/title companies ask are:

- Who are the trustees/trustors?
- Who are the successor trustees?
- Who are the beneficiaries?
- What is supposed to happen upon the death of the trustees/trustors?

The answers to these questions guide us through the transaction. These answers can only be found in the trust. Upon the death of the trustors/trustees, the title/escrow companies will need to see a copy of the trust and all amendments to the trust (if any).

The Problem with the Poor Man's Will

A common occurrence in holding title to real estate is what I call the "Poor Man's Will". Instead of creating a will or a trust which will be a better method of holding title, the homeowner adds their son or daughter on to title of the property. The thought process is often "that way someone is able to take care of things should something happen to me." While I commend them for thinking about the inevitable, there can be some issues with doing this.

Here is a scenario where this didn't work out in their favor:

The parent bought the property 30 years ago for a $50,000 and now because of California' exorbitant real estate prices the home is worth $600,000. The homeowner years earlier had added their son to the property. When the homeowner died and the son sold the property he was left with a $550,000 capital gain and more importantly capital gains taxes (this is an estimate of the amount, because of course there were improvements added to the basis, selling costs deducted from the sales price, etc.). The son was not expecting that and hopefully he found a good tax preparer to help him with that issue. With the state and federal rates totaling over 25% in California, plus any depreciation recapture (if it was depreciated for business use or rental property), the son was facing quite a hefty tax bill! By adding the son to the title of the property, the homeowner passed their cost basis on to the son.

Conversely, had the homeowner set up a trust and passed the property through the trust (or even through probate); the heir would have received a stepped up basis. With a stepped up basis in the above scenario there would be no capital gains and no taxes due. In other words, when the owner died the property is worth $600,000. The heir inherits it at this value. It is sold for $600,000. Therefore, acquired at $600,000, sold for $600,000…no capital gain. Remember, this is not a tax book, consult your own tax advisor! ☺

Another issue I have seen with this "Poor Man's Will" has to do with liens of the person added to title. I have been involved in numerous transactions where the parents added an adult child to the title of their property. The reason again, in case something happens to them the child will have an easy way to distribute the property to the other siblings. However, while the parents are still alive, they want to refinance. The adult child that was added to the property had a child support lien recorded against them that is now attached to the property. This lien has to be paid or otherwise released before the parents can refinance. The parents were not prepared for this lien on the property and it turned out to be a very challenging situation.

The last issue I will mention came from a phone call. A client of mine, a real estate agent, called with his client, John, on the phone. John's brother, Tim, was the adult child added to the title prior to the death of the parents. John and the other siblings were having difficulty dealing with Tim. After the parents were gone, Tim felt like he was king of the castle and everyone had to play by the tune of his drum! Again, another very challenging situation.

Many scenarios like these over the years have led me to believe that the best option is to talk with a good estate planning attorney and put a plan in place that will minimize these types of issues. The TOD deed which is available in many states is often a good solution. After January 1, 2016 in California, it will be interesting to see the use of this new deed in the state.

Receiving the Property Out of Probate or Out of a Trust

I was working on a case several years back where the property was distributed via final decree and distribution (out of probate) to four siblings. I believe there were several properties as well as cash investments and other items that were distributed. In this situation there was an issue that came up after the distribution from the estate. The property was distributed to all 4 of the siblings, and then 3 of them proceeded to deed over to one of the siblings. The issue with this is that transfers from parents or from the estate of the parent to the child is not a re-assessable event by the tax assessor. If you read the California revenue and tax code transfers from parent to child are not a change in ownership. There is a form you fill out that prevents a re-assessment of the property (contact the assessor regarding props. 58 & 193). However, when the property transferred from the

3 siblings to the 1 sibling, it constituted a change in ownership and therefore a re-assessable event.

Transfers between siblings are considered changes of ownership in the California revenue and tax code and therefore they re-assess the property. In this case, the assessor reassessed ¾ of the property. Four children received the property from the parent's estate (no re-assessment) then 3 of the siblings deeded it over to the 1 sibling and in doing so caused a re-assessment.

This came as a big surprise to the family and caused a huge increase in their annual tax bill. At times there is a reason property is distributed from an estate in a certain way. However, in this situation, they frankly didn't consider the re-assessment and in the end they paid for it.

An equally damaging issue that can present itself when property is distributed to the heirs of an estate is the attachment of liens to property. I was dealing with a similar estate where there also happened to be 4 or 5 siblings inheriting a property. The siblings receive their property from the estate through a final decree and distribution, and subsequently sold the property. The issue was that one of the siblings had a child support lien and some judgments. The moment that person took title to the property via the final decree and distribution those liens attached to that property and had to be paid off in order to complete the sale. Those liens delayed the closing of the transaction. Additionally, those liens totaled more than that sibling's share of the property. What a dilemma!

Obviously, those of us in real estate reading this passage will know this is not a scenario that we want to have. In order to complete the sale, they had to negotiate with the creditors and create some alternative solutions to a normal sale of property. If the ultimate goal was to sell the property, why didn't they have the estate sell the property and split the proceeds amongst the siblings? This would have made for a much smoother real estate transaction and less headaches.

The ultimate message here...consider all the possibilities prior to distributing the property from the estate. And of course, obtain proper legal advice! ☺

An Extremely Costly Mistake on Deeds

A very costly mistake that I have seen made over and over in the last 20 years is deeding a property to an entity or person that has no ability or capacity to deed out of title. It is kind of like the 2nd Gulf War. It was easy to get into, yet hard to get out of!

I have seen this in various ways. Let's examine them:

1. A deed to an individual or entity that either doesn't exist or is not in good standing with the state in which it was formed. I am not sure what the reason, but it is far too common that people deed to an entity that does not exist. Maybe it is because they haven't filed the entity paperwork with the state, but they are planning to do so? Maybe it is because they are trying to hide the asset or take it out of a person's name for a variety of reasons and have limited time so they

just make it up? Maybe the entity did exist at some point, but no longer exists? Whatever the reason, it causes a big problem and usually requires a court order in order to take it out of that name or entity. If the entity is real, but was just not in good standing with the state it was formed in, one just has to bring it back into good standing before transactions can be acted upon.

2. A deed to a person that does not have capacity to act. I recently was working on a file in which the borrower on the transaction wanted to be in title with an elderly person who was incapacitated. I cannot imagine the reason they wanted to be in title with an incapacitated person. What if they need to sell the property at some point? What if they want to refinance it or take out another mortgage? Their options will be limited because they will not be able to obtain signatures of the person who is incapacitated. This would force them into a situation where they have to go to the probate courts and obtain conservatorship in order to do a transaction.

3. A deed to a minor. Minors do not have the legal capacity to act on a real estate transaction. I have seen this far too many times in my career and it perplexes me every time. Well, not every time...in one situation it was apparent that one ex-spouse was taking revenge on the other by deeding the property to the child instead of the former spouse. Whatever the motivation, it results in either waiting until the minor turns 18, or obtaining guardianship from the probate courts.

4. A deed to a trust...not the trustee of the trust. Entities like LLCs or corporations can hold title in the exact name of the LLC or corporation. Trusts however cannot. Trustees of the trust

must hold title. It is too common that we find properties held in the "the John Doe Family Trust" instead of "John Doe as trustee of the John Doe Family Trust dtd...". This is a vital mistake and the deed to the trust (rather than the trustee of the trust) is not valid.

Many of these mistakes end up with a court order to correct them. In some circumstances we can figure out a "work-around" or solve the problem in some other way. The majority end up in court to correct the errors. Hopefully, if many people read this information we can stop the cycle of madness!

I often receive "The Call" with a problem as a result of wrong deeds after the fact...after the deed has been executed, notarized and recorded. Once the deed has recorded, the problem is there. You cannot un-ring the bell. You cannot just say "Do over!" like when we were kids. Contact a title expert or attorney BEFORE recording the deeds to ensure you are doing the right thing.

The second aspect of these deed mistakes is deeding real property to people or entities that have liens against them. Most people do not realize that certain liens attach to individuals or entities and EVERY property that the individual or entity owns. The mistake that is made over and over again is: properties are deeded to individuals or entities that have state or federal tax liens, child support liens, judgments, etc. These liens then attach to the property and become liens that must be paid in order to sell, refinance or obtain a loan on the property.

Case Study

Over 10 years ago a woman was trying to sell her property. About 2 years earlier she had become behind on her mortgage payments and went to a person who "helped" her stop the foreclosure of her property. The way they did it was by adding someone to the title to her property, and that person filed bankruptcy. Two years after that, when she was trying to sell the property she had a very rude awakening. The gentleman that was added to her title had a child support lien and she had to pay it in order to sell the property!

Case Study

A person deeds their family member onto title of a property. Later the same day they deed the family member off title. Months later, during their refinance they realize that the family member's liens stay on the property. Those liens must be paid in order to sell, refinance or obtain a loan on the property!

Like I said earlier, people often call me AFTER the problem is already there. These two cases are exactly what I was referring to! *Prior* to deeding someone or some entity onto your title, you must consider the consequences of doing so. Call an expert before you make this crucial mistake and always obtain legal and tax advice!

Agent/Investor Tip!!

Add value by helping your clients avoid the mistakes discussed in this chapter (and every other chapter for that matter)! Remember that you cannot "un-ring" a bell. Once a deed or transfer records with the county recorder…the damage may already be done. We cannot always fix the problems afterwards without going to court.

Chapter 7 Trust Sale Process

Although this is a book on probate, since trusts fall under the same section of law, it is important that we discuss trust sales as well. Most trust sales are regular sales. These are not to be confused with Trustee's Sales, which are actually foreclosures by the lender in Deed of Trust states (states that use deeds of trust to secure loans instead of mortgages and therefore foreclose via trustee's sales rather than judicial foreclosures). The trust sale refers to any property where title is held by a trust and the trustee (or successor trustee) of the trust is the seller.

Normally, people refer to trust sales when the original grantors/trustors/owners have passed away and are selling the property. If John Doe created the John Doe family trust then later sells the property; that is not what people are normally referring to when they say it is a trust sale. However, when John Doe dies and his daughter Sally Doe, the successor trustee is selling; then we are referring to it as a trust sale.

One of the most important things to know when dealing with a trust sale is that a complete copy of the trust and all amendments needs to be provided to the title company. It is that document that tells us who is the successor trustee(s) (the party that has powers to act on behalf of the trust in place of the original trustee who has passed away or become incapacitated), what powers they have to act, who the beneficiaries are and what is supposed to happen to the property upon death of the trustor/grantor/owner.

As long as the actions of the seller are within the guidelines of the trust document, trust sales are usually quite easy and just like a regular sale. The trustee has very significant responsibilities legally and it is recommended that they receive consultation from an attorney before they carry out their duties. This can often be an opportunity for an agent or investor to give a referral to an attorney!

Lost Trust

When the trust document is lost and the successor trustee cannot find the copy of the trust, there is a big problem. As mentioned above, the trust document governs the powers of the successor trustee and who is named successor trustee as well as a lot of other key information. Without it, how will anyone know what is supposed to happen upon death of the trustor? When the trust document is unavailable, the successor trustees will generally have to see a judge. They should consult an attorney and let the attorney guide them on how to deal with that situation.

Court Confirmation for Protection

In some cases, a trust sale that could normally be completed without any intervention from the court is done via court confirmation. Usually this is done in order to protect the trustee from claims of the beneficiaries but there could potentially be other reasons. The trustee, usually in consultation with the attorney, can elect to have a court confirmation sale

and have the court oversee the whole process. (See Chapter 4)

See also Heggstad in Chapter 5.

Can I Do a Probate Short Sale?

A probate short sale…if that's not two things that can create extra paperwork, extra challenges on the transaction, then I don't know what it is! But the question is, why would you do that? Why would you sell a short sale that is a probate or probate that is a short sale? Why would you do that? There has to be some benefit in it for the estate and for the beneficiaries. If not, they would just let it go to foreclosure.

Benefits

Let's examine potential benefits of a probate short sale. First of all, I worked on a case where selling the property to one of the tenants was the dying wish of the decedent. This can be a big one. The estate administrator in this case said, "I know my relative wanted to do this, so I want to complete this for them." So they decided to sell that property via short sale to that person.

Another reason could be liens on the property. There may be liens on the property and in order to clear those liens they wish to short sell the property. They may get a negotiated amount on those liens and clear them from other claims against the estate. That way those liens do not make a claim on other assets in the estate. That is a huge reason to do a short sale and I've worked with situations where the attorney advised his clients to short sell the property.

Another reason…move out money. Lenders may pay $3,000- $5,000 as move out money or "cash for keys".

Lenders do this to avoid the foreclosure process. So the move out money could be the way to turn an asset that's worth nothing (because it's worth less than what is owed on it) into an asset that can generate some funds for the estate or a specific heir living in the property.

One more reason is to sell the property to a relative. Most short sales must be "arm's length" transactions. In other words, the seller must not know the buyer. Because the sale is a probate, the lender will often allow "non-arm's length" transactions in which the buyer and seller are relatives.

The real question on a probate short sale is how do you pay for the attorney's fees? Generally speaking there is no money to the seller or to the estate in the short sale. The answer is that either the bank will cover the fees, or the buyer, or the agents...or a combination of all three.

I had one transaction that was such a good deal for the buyer that they had no problem contributing a few thousand dollars to pay for attorney's fees. I have had other transactions where the bank really did not want the property back so they were glad that it was going to be a short sale.   The bank contributed some money and instead of paying a couple thousand dollars for a second mortgage, the bank paid a couple thousand dollars for the attorney's fees. In other circumstances, I've seen agents commit a portion of their commission to help pay for attorney's fees. Sometimes you have to do what you have to do to get the sale to go through! As mentioned previously, search for a good reason for the estate to go through with the short sale.

Six Good Reasons for a Probate Short Sale

Let's review six good reasons for a probate short sale. There are various reasons why one might want to do a probate short sale and these are the most compelling reasons I've seen.

1. To clear liens from the estate. I had a client who was working on a probate that had several properties in it. A couple of the properties were worth less than they owed the bank, but some of the other properties had equity. The attorney advised the administrator to sell the properties that were "under water" (short sales) in order to settle all the liens so that they would not have any claim on the rest of the estate.

2. To fulfill the dying wish of the decedent. The decedent may have, before they died, wanted to sell that property to a certain tenant or a certain relative. It is not uncommon that people want to ultimately see a certain person have their property. The administrator may want to do a short sale to fulfill that wish.

3. To reduce the total expenses paid out of other assets of the estate. The estate will pay for attorney fees, administrator fees, court fees and other miscellaneous fees. By doing a short sale you may have some of those fees paid out of the sale of the property. Because the property is worth less than what is owed to the bank, you are essentially paying the fees out of the bank's proceeds. That is much better than paying fees out of a bank account or some other monies that may be in the estate.

4. To receive "move-out" money. In some cases, banks are still doing move out money or cash for keys on short sales. This will turn a property that has no real value to the estate into a small amount of cash to the estate.

5. To make a good deal. Sometimes the short sale price is such a great deal for the buyer that the buyer is willing to pay extra for the property to cover

expenses, attorney fees, etc. It could be that the property is priced as an extreme value. It could be that there is so much demand for homes in a particular area (which we have been experiencing over the last few years). Whatever the reason, if the buyer wants to contribute to the estate administration fees, let them!

6. To sell to a family member. One of the only "non-arm's length" transactions allowed in the short sale world is when there is a deceased party. A probate short sale is an excellent way to transfer the property to a family member at fair market value.

Can You Pay the Administrator/Executor on a Short Sale?

Often, the executor/administrator will be a little hesitant about having the property sold. They may not think it is worth selling the house because the property is worth less than what is owed to the bank. But as I will point out in the pages that follow (see California Probate Code Section 11420) fees are owed to them for their services. The executor/administrator takes care of all the responsibilities of the probate. If their fee is on the closing disclosure for the transaction (formerly the HUD-1), they could and should be paid.

The same applies for the attorney and their fees. They are due their fee for the responsibilities and duties that they performed during the probate process. Most importantly, all fees for the administrator and attorney must be on the closing disclosure when submitted to the bank. It doesn't mean the bank will approve them, but if they are not on the closing disclosure, you have no shot!

As one agent put it, "And you know the nice thing about it Kevin, was they were so happy that the home that their beloved person had lived in is going to a family that is going to love and cherish that home just the way they did. And they don't have the last memory of the home being a foreclosure on their record."

Pay the Administrator (Probate Code 11420)

There is a little known fact about the probate code that can help real estate agents with their probate short sales. Most people haven't read <u>Probate Code 11420</u>. This section of the probate code helps us on probate short sales. It indicates that estate administration expenses related to the administration of the property are to be paid out before the loans that are secured on that property. To be exact, it states that:

"Debts shall be paid in the following order of priority.....

(1) Expenses of administration. With respect to obligations secured by mortgage, deed of trust, or other lien, including, but not limited to, a judgment lien, only those expenses of administration incurred that are reasonably related to the administration of that property by which obligations are secured shall be given priority over these obligations."

Hmmm...who knew the estate expenses for dealing with the property take priority over the mortgages.

In other words, if you have an estate where there is only one asset wouldn't all the expenses for administration be for that one asset...or even in other cases where there are multiple assets, the expenses for that asset should be paid prior to the mortgage or deed of trust. That is useful information, because that gives you fire power when dealing with a short sale to get the bank to approve the sale with money going to the administrator or money going to the attorney.

What this means to us is that apparently, banks should not be getting paid first! The attorney's fees and executor/administrator's fees should come first and be approved without change on the closing disclosure. Since not many people know this, it may be a good idea to submit a copy of <u>Probate Code 11420</u> along with your short sale package and closing disclosure. Use this info and take control of your transactions!

The second thing this means to us is that agents should have leverage for obtaining more Probate Short Sale listings! You can use this information to help heirs understand that even though the decedent's house is worth less than what is owed on the loan, the executor/administrator may collect thousands of dollars in fees for the administration of the estate.

Of course the bank always has the right to accept or reject any short sale. The bank has the right to place whatever terms they desire on the short sale. But this information may be invaluable in the situations where it works to put money from the short sale in the pocket of the administrator or executor.

Agent/Investor Tip!!

1. The bank considers the net dollars. That net figure determines what they will allow. For that reason, there is wide variation (even within the same lender) in what they will accept, pay for, etc.

2. Properties in a poor disposition that the bank does not want back (via foreclosure) may help you get your

short sale approved. If the property needs a lot of work, has termites, mold or other toxic substances, water damage, smoke or fire damage, bad tenants, etc. the bank may want to do everything possible to avoid a foreclosure. Naturally, that will also affect whether or not they pay attorney's fees, accept certain offers, etc.

3. The negotiator for the bank is normally not a management level employee. I'll bet even their manager doesn't know about probate code 11420. Use that to your advantage whenever possible.

Chapter 9 How Much Does Probate Cost?

In the normal course of business I often hear this question: "How much will probate cost?" I thought it would be appropriate to shed some light on this subject!

Court Fees

First and foremost, there are court fees that must be paid for the probate. The fees run approximately $400 to file the probate petition and approximately another $400 to file the petition for final distribution of the estate assets (at the time of this writing). There are also often miscellaneous fees for things like publication of notices, probate referee fees (typically about .1 % of the assets appraised), and fees for certified copies of documents. Some attorneys estimate $1,500 to $2,500 in court fees and miscellaneous costs.

Estate Representative/Attorney Fees

California Probate Code § 10810 sets the maximum fees that attorneys and personal representatives can charge for a probate. The personal representative is the executor or administrator. The personal representative may or may not choose to charge fees depending on the circumstances. One consideration for the personal representative is if they are also a beneficiary. If so, they have to decide whether it is better to receive fees (potentially taxable income) and a reduced estate for all the beneficiaries as opposed to just receiving their inheritance (potentially non-taxable). The decision should be made with the consultation of their legal advisor and certified tax planner or CPA. **They will probably consider the amounts they will receive if fees are taken out of the estate before splitting the inheritance with the other beneficiaries, as opposed to just splitting the whole pie with the beneficiaries. The results can be different in each case.**

Typically, personal representatives *AND* attorneys can charge 4% of the first $100,000 of the estate, 3% of the next $100,000, 2% of the next $800,000, 1% of the next $9,000,000, and ½ % of the next $15,000,000. For estates larger than $25,000,000, the court will determine the fee for the amount that is greater than $25,000,000. (Not knowing the fees on an estate larger than $25,000,000 is a very good problem to have!)

Value of Estate	Cost
First $100,000	4%
Next $100,000	3%
Next $800,000	2%
Next $9,000,000	1%
Next $15,000,000	1/2%
Estates larger than $25,000,000	TBD by the court

In special circumstances or complicated cases, higher fees can be approved by the courts.

Here is a chart of the total basic charges:

Value of Estate	Compensation to Attorney and/or Personal Representative under the Probate Code
$100,000	$4,000
$200,000	$7,000
$300,000	$9,000
$400,000	$11,000
$500,000	$13,000
$600,000	$15,000
$700,000	$17,000
$800,000	$19,000
$900,000	$21,000
$1,000,000	$23,000
$1,500,000	$28,000
$2,000,000	$33,000
$3,000,000	$43,000
$5,000,000	$63,000
$10,000,000	$113,000
$15,000,000	$138,000
$20,000,000	$163,000

Remember, these are the amounts that both the attorney AND the personal representatives can charge. The actual payments could be double what you see in the charts (if both the attorney and the PR are charging these amounts). Also note that these charges can only be charged once the court has ordered the fees paid from the estate. This usually happens at the end of the probate process as part of the final accounting. This is a very important point.

Many times I have seen heirs to an estate procrastinating on filing the probate of the estate because they don't have any money. The fact is, the fees out of pocket are minimal and some attorneys will even advance the out of pocket fees and be reimbursed by the estate. In most circumstances, the fees for the probate will be paid out of the proceeds of the estate....not the pocket of the heirs nor executors.

Value of the Estate

Estates are appraised by probate referees, who are appointed by the State Controller to determine the fair market value of the asset. The value of the asset (and therefore the amount for calculating the attorney's or PR's fees) does not take into consideration the amount of debts or liens on the property.

For example:
A home is worth $500,000 but has a loan balance of $480,000. There is, therefore, $20,000 of equity. However, the amount used for calculating the value of the estate and therefore the attorney's or PR's fees would be $500,000 which is the value of the home.

Horror Story

A client of mine called me and I spoke with their actual seller. The seller proceeded to explain that the attorney she talked to asked for a $35,000 retainer on an estate valued at about $400,000. I do not know how that could even be within the law, but that is what the attorney asked for. Proof that it is often good to obtain a second opinion!

Probate Can Be Free

The costs and fees of probate and probate laws, especially in real estate, can intimidate many people and keep them from going through the process. Probate costs can be up to 4 percent of the total value of assets, plus court fees and other costs. But for low-income persons you can actually have all your probate costs and fees waived. Because of probate laws that are currently in place, going through probate court can actually be totally free.

This is no small matter. Probate costs and fees include court fees, personal representation fees and lawyers' fees. All of these fees depend on where you live. They are the same throughout California, except for in Riverside, San Bernardino and San Francisco counties, where fees can also include a small surcharge related to local court construction needs (as of the date this was written). Court fees can be as low as a few hundred dollars or as high as a few thousand. If you're dealing with real estate in probate court you can expect those fees to start piling up. So how do you get the probate court fees waived?

If a person can prove to the court that they are a low-income person and cannot afford to pay the fee to file the court papers, they can ask for a fee waiver. There are 3 ways to qualify for a fee waiver:

1. If one is receiving public aid like Medi-Cal, Food Stamps (EBT), Cal-Works, General Assistance, SSI, SSP, Tribal TANF, IHHS or CAPI.

2. If one's household income, before taxes, is less than the amounts listed on Form FW-001 in item 5b (LINK - http://www.courts.ca.gov/documents/fw001.pdf). It's around $1,150 for one person, $2,400 for a family of four.

3. If the court finds that a person does not have enough income to pay for their household's basic needs AND the court fees.

If one meets the above conditions and wants to have their fees waived they need to take a few more steps. One should follow instructions on the Information Sheet on Waiver of Superior Court Fees and Costs (Form FW-001-INFO) and Request to Waive Court Fees (Form FW-001). Fee waivers expire 60 days after your case is closed, whether that is by a judgment, a dismissal, or in some other way. They can also end if the court finds that you are no longer eligible for the fee waiver.

How much value can you provide to a potential client/seller by having this information?

Agent/Investor Tip!

I had a client call me with a seller that was ready willing and able to sell a property. The property was free and clear so there was a couple hundred thousand dollars of equity. The problem was that the heirs had no money to pay for a probate (if I had a dollar for every time that has been true!). They were "property rich" and "cash poor". They were holding back from doing anything with the estate, for many years, because they didn't have any money. This is a big mistake that far too many people make. The longer you wait to probate a property, the more headaches that arise.

Fortunately, for this client, there are some attorneys that can take on a case with little or no money up front. It is quite risky for the attorney, but I have seen it done many times. In some cases the attorney will advance the court fees and misc. expenses so there is zero out of pocket for the person filing the probate case. In this case, the attorney took the case with little or no money up front. The attorney mentioned to me "I cannot legally collect a fee until ordered by the judge anyway (at the closing of the estate), so I can help them out". This resulted in a closed listing for the agent, and fees paid to the attorney from the profits of the sale.

Find and *CHERISH* attorneys like this!!

How to Avoid the 10 Most Common Mistakes in Probate Real Estate

I just recently closed a real estate transaction that was quite troubling. It was one of those deals that took over a year to close; they were in and out of court and had to change the court orders several times. While I know these things happen, this one just made no sense to me because it was all preventable.

You see, after working on this case for more than 8 months the agent brought me in to help with title matters (finally they brought in a specialist). It was good that they brought me in when they did because additional mistakes would have been made if they hadn't. If they had the right team involved to begin with, they could have possibly closed the transaction 6 months earlier or more!

For that reason I have created a list of the 10 most common mistakes in probate real estate that can kill your deal (or delay it unmercifully). Take note of these as this information will directly impact your business!

1. Not checking for personal liens that the decedent may have had. Especially, in today's economy it is becoming more common to find liens, judgments, child and spousal support and other personal matters that affect the property held by the decedent. Rather than letting these things become a problem that "pops up" at the end of the transaction, why not resolve the problem at the beginning of the escrow, or better yet, when you first take the listing! This is not hard to do...in fact, all you have to do is call

a good probate specialist and they will take care of it for you.

2. Not checking for old liens against the property that may need to be cleared. The law says that lien holders must release liens that are paid-off within a certain time period (depending on the type of lien). In a perfect world (violin playing in the background), we would all abide by the law, wouldn't we. But unfortunately....the people in this world are not perfect. For that reason, there are often old loans, judgments and other encumbrances that according to the homeowners "were taken care of years ago". However, when a title search is done, it reveals that the public record still shows those items attached to the property.

   These liens must be taken care of prior to closing a sale to a new owner. It is often more difficult to deal with these issues when the owner or borrower is deceased because the heirs may not have any information about the liens, lien payments or anything. The more time you have the better chance you have of resolving these issues and not delaying your closing date. It would make better sense to begin dealing with these issues early in the process, wouldn't it?

3. Delays in court procedures, filing documents, and obtaining documents from the court. Depending on the type of transaction and probate case you are working on, the documents needed to close the transaction can vary quite dramatically. In some cases, the documents needed to close are given by the court up front; in other cases not until the end of the court proceedings. Either way, wouldn't you want to know what is needed and when it is

available? Wouldn't you want to provide those documents to the companies that can facilitate the closing at the earliest possible time? This is a very important step in the process and I have seen agents who didn't avoid this pitfall wait months to close their transactions.

4. Delays in reviewing the documents related to the probate. Once the documents are received from the court they should be sent to escrow AND title immediately so that they can be reviewed. Just because there is a court order doesn't mean everything is resolved and ready to go. There are many cases in which court orders have mistakes, errors or omissions, or are just downright written incorrectly. Sending the documents to your closing agents right away can save you headaches in the end. Bonus Tip: To be completely proactive and get one step ahead of the rest, ask the attorney to let a probate specialist at the title company review the court order PRIOR to submitting it to the judge for approval and signature. Just recently a client of mine was able to save a 2nd trip back to court by letting me suggest an edit to the court order they were planning to have the judge sign.

5. The closing agent or escrow officer, not being proactive in coordinating between the title company, beneficiaries, and the attorney/courts. This is not to single out escrow officers, there are plenty of really good ones out there. It is just that they are such a crucial and important part of any transaction. Having an escrow officer that has experience closing probate transactions is so very important.

Before I continue with the list I have to mention a deal that I closed not long ago. In fact, it was the first deal from a new attorney and it really made me look good!

I don't want to sound like I am bashing my competitors, but it was a deal in which another title company told the attorney that they would have to wait 60 days after the court order was signed before they could close their transaction. Well, I don't know about you, but I would have had 2 mortgage payments due in those 60 days. If I were the agent it would not have been fun waiting for my commission check because the deal had not closed.

You see, every title company has their own preferences for types of transactions, likes and dislikes and well...you get the picture. For me and the company I work for, we favor the probates, trust, estates, guardianships and conservatorships. That is exactly why on the same transaction that "brand X" title said they would have to wait 60 days, we were able to close immediately after receiving the court order. You can't beat that for service can you? Yes that was a shameless plug!

6. The title company not being proactive in working with the escrow, beneficiaries, and the attorney/courts. The preceding example says it all about title companies and what they will/won't do and what they can/can't do. Because of past experience and/or preferences of the management at other companies, you may receive more restrictive requirements in order to close your transaction. Therefore, it is imperative that you work with a specialist in this area.

7. Not having a knowledgeable title representative that can coordinate (see 3, 4, and 5) when necessary. Let's refresh:

3. Delays in proceedings, filing documents and obtaining documents from the court.

4. Delays in reviewing those documents.

5. The escrow officer not being proactive in coordinating between title, beneficiaries, and the attorney/courts. And don't forget the bonus tip: having the court orders reviewed before they are submitted to the judge. This may not always be possible, but if you can pull it off...it is a good thing. A good title company will not give you overly restrictive requirements and will fight to make the transaction go as quickly as possible.

8. Unwillingness of any of the involved parties to work together to achieve the closed transaction (title companies, escrow, attorneys, beneficiaries, etc.). At times it is hard to get the parties to work together to achieve the common goal....a closed transaction. Sometimes this is the hardest part. Thank goodness for those psychology classes in college.
Sometimes you will act as a therapist, manager, coach, helper, assistant, real estate agent, or anything else. The goal is to get to the closing table as quickly and simply as possible. There have been countless occasions in which I have been summoned to call Mr. Smith the borrower, attorney, seller, agent, cousin, etc. because someone needs to talk some sense to them. I welcome the opportunity to go the extra mile to get the deal closed. You should too!

9. Original documents not provided to the title/escrow company for recording. Sometimes, clients provide plain copies of documents when what is needed is an original wet signature or certified copy. For the most part, court orders are documents that we must record at closing. Therefore, we must have an original (wet signature) or certified copy (with the certified stamp on it). *See the Chapters 3 and 4 on Court Conf/Non conf*

for details about which documents are required to be certified copies or originals.

10. Court orders that limit your ability to close. Indicating a lender name, loan type, loan amount, etc. on court orders is not a good idea since these things may change. Conversely, other portions of the court order being too vague are another problem. At the closing table, we cannot make assumptions. Court orders need to be explicit when indicating who is receiving title, who is to receive payment, etc. This may seem obvious, but I have seen many court orders that were written in a way that was very confusing. We must follow the court order "to the letter", so if that order is not clear, it makes it difficult when it is time to close the transaction.

Attorneys write the court orders and give them to the judge to sign. Therefore, different case, different attorney, different court order language. This can be hard to deal with when trying to close a real estate transaction. On challenging transactions it is a good idea to have the title company review the court order before it is presented to the judge for signature.

Agent/Investor Tip!! *(The Real #1 Mistake in Probate Real Estate)*

The biggest mistake agents and investors make in probate real estate is not developing a system to go after probate sales. It can be a steady flow of business that can pay you for years to come. The key is to systematize your lead generation so that you can create this steady flow rock solid, reliable business. Your database of attorneys can become as reliable a source of referrals and therefore closed commissions, as your rental income on investment properties.

An outstanding system to set up for your probate marketing can be found at www.ProbateRealEstateSales101.com.

Chapter 11 Marketing

Investing In Probate Properties

Probate Investing is the "best" lead source for finding residential real estate! Within the first 4-6 months of the estate administration more than 45% of the Estate Executors/Administrators will sell property in the estate. The best advice is to market newly filed probate cases early and often.

In the past 22 years in this business I have seen some of the most amazing deals come out of probate real estate sales. Some years ago I was speaking with the representative of an estate who was dealing with a property. He lived a few hundred miles away from the property and had 4 siblings. After we discussed several issues he was dealing with, he said "I really just want this whole process over with! Heck, sell the house for $450,000....sell it for $400,000. It doesn't matter to me I just want to be done."

The opportunity with probate real estate stems from the fact that the seller that you are dealing with is not the person who lived in the property, built it, made the improvements, loved the home for the last 15 years, etc. In the case of this gentleman, he was a busy, successful career person and was splitting the proceeds of the property with 4 other people. At $450,000 he would net about $50,000 and at $400,000 he would net about $40,000. That difference of $10,000 was nowhere near the value of having the headache be over. Wouldn't you like to be the investor/agent negotiating on the other end of that sale?

How to Find the Leads

Lead generation is very important when it comes to probate real estate (and real estate in general for that matter). When the Patriot Act was put in place, it limited access to certain death records. However, there are still several ways to obtain information about prospective probate listings. The information you will want to know is the next of kin and/or heirs, and the attorney's information if there is one involved. If there is a probate case started, you will want to know who filed the petition and/or who is appointed to be in charge of the estate.

Here are a few different ways to obtain probate leads:

- Attorneys—They can be a great source of probate leads, not just today but in the future. In fact, attorneys can almost be like a stream of residual income (not quite, but close). If you are able to establish excellent relationships with attorneys and provide outstanding service to their clients, they will continue to come back to you.

- Probate Courts—Going to the courthouse can be time consuming and arduous in some areas. However, all the records are there. Most court houses allow you to view the files and records for free and even make copies for a nominal charge (or you can take pictures with your phone for free). Some counties have this information available online. I know that San Diego County allows you to purchase copies of documents in the file online and I believe Sacramento and some other counties in Northern California do as well. Check your local county's website to find out what information is available.

- Obituaries—Often the first public place you can find out about a death is in the obituaries in local newspapers. Now when you read that John Doe in Anytown, CA passed away it is easy to search online to find out if he had a home. This may not always be exactly accurate because many people have similar names. However, you will often find that there are only a handful of people with a similar name in the same city. Using obituaries may make you feel like an ambulance chaser...so using tact is extremely important here. No passing out business cards at funerals!!!

- Online Services—In many areas, there are lead generation companies that actually provide probate case filing information on their websites as probate leads. Their fees typically range from $25-$100 per month. This makes it easier to find individuals who have filed probate cases.

- Churches—For many families, the first call upon the death of a loved one is to their pastor, priest, rabbi, etc. Creating the relationship with the religious organization may be the challenge, but once established, the pastor can refer people who have experienced a death but have real estate to deal with to you. This can prove to be an extremely good referral. You can help a family in need while providing your real estate service at the same time.

There are many other sources for probate leads and lead generation. In fact, very soon I will be coming out with a complete system for contacting estate representatives and attorneys and making your probate real estate business an awesome lead generating machine that pays you over and over and over again! Stay tuned for updates at www.ProbateRealEstateSales101.com

How/When Do I Contact The Executor/Administrator?

It is impossible to specify the best time to contact an executor/administrator! This is a trying time and each executor/administrator will respond differently. Be mindful of what they are going through: the death of a loved one, being in charge of a process that can seem overwhelming, dealing with potentially several family members (some of whom may not be the easiest to deal with), being responsible for money/assets that they have never dealt with before or may not own themselves, living out of the area while trying to manage a new process...the list goes on and on. Be compassionate, empathetic and courteous.

Since there is no best time...just do it! The Key is to communicate with executor/administrator frequently:

- Keep a mailing in front of them often. At least every other week or so.
- Stop by to see them. Door knocking is great. It is common that the agent/investor that knocks on the door is the one that gets the deal. You stand out from the rest if you take the time to go see them.
- Call them. Most of the time you won't have the phone number for the estate representative. The agents and investors who take the time to search for their phone numbers are one step ahead.
- Drive by the property and "keep an eye on things".
- This is your lead – reach out to them every couple of weeks (or more often...just don't become a burden).
- If you do not get the response you want in one mailing – wait a couple of weeks and try again.
- Add Value. Check out www.ProbateRealEstateSales101.com for creative ways to add value.
- Be consistent. 45% of probate cases sell in the first 4-6 months. That means there are still several that will sell later! Some also complete the probate process and then the people who inherited the property sell right after the probate case is over.

Remember, time has a way of making an executor/administrator more responsive to a realistic offer. The same seller that is appalled by your $300,000 offer in February may jump at it in November! Staying consistent and following-up will be crucial. It is common that sellers, heirs and probate estates lower their price expectations after they have dealt with the property for a while. Investors with a lower cash sale that can close quickly are more attractive after months or years of dealing with a problem property.

Reach out to as many executors/administrators as possible – there are no "magic bullets" here. Systematize your approach to get the best results…especially when it comes to follow-up. This will take work on your part. Answer these questions: How will I differentiate myself from all of the other agents and investors that are contacting this estate representative? Why should the executor/administrator talk to me? Why should the executor/administrator consider my offer? What added value do I bring to the table?

You may reach an executor/administrator that tells you that this property is no longer available. Move on to the next one, but don't forget to revisit this person at a later date. Again, systematize your approach to get the best results. Remember every executor/administrator is different and will respond differently to various marketing attempts. The key is to fish with a big net!

Finding Cash Investors

Having a large list of Cash Investors can be an incredible resource for your real estate career; whether you are an investor or an agent. Prior to reading this, if you did not have a list such as this, then this is a great opportunity for you. This list can be invaluable when marketing to probate properties.

You will have a unique position when you have a database of cash buyers for the property. Within 2-3 days after reading this, it is your own fault if you do not have a list such as this! Stop reading now and call your title company!!

A good title company can obtain a list of cash buyers for you within days if not hours. Talk to your title company representative and request the list. Then contact the individuals and entities on the list and start creating a database. Many if not all of those cash buyers are professional buyers that are always looking for deals. You now have a list of professional buyers (and sellers) that you can begin incorporating into your probate real estate business.

For more information on Marketing and creating a system to continuously obtain probate listings, go to www.ProbateRealEstateSales101.com.

Chapter 12 Case Studies and Q & A

Case Studies

The seller died while we were in escrow. What do we do now?

A while back I was working on a transaction in which the seller passed away prior to the close of escrow. The seller had signed the listing agreement, the escrow paperwork, the grant deed; everything that was necessary to close the transaction. Everything was moving along quite well in the transaction. After traveling out of state to return home, the seller passed away prior to the close of escrow.

What do you do in this case? Does it now become a probate situation? Can you close the real estate transaction?

Well, a grant deed is legal upon "delivery"- the act of unconditionally sending or giving the deed to the grantee, or in this case to the escrow. Because the deed (and all other documents for the transaction) had been delivered, we were able to close the transaction without probating the estate. The key here is that ALL paperwork that needed to be signed by the seller had already been signed and delivered.

I have worked on several other cases in which a seller has passed away while in escrow but has not signed and delivered all documents necessary. In those cases, the family, heirs, or estate have had to make other arrangements for the sale depending on the presence of a trust, will or other estate planning tools.

Are inherited properties considered community property?

A few years ago I worked on a transaction in which a person died and left real property to their daughter through the probate of their estate. An issue came up when the husband of the daughter was found to have liens that would attach to the property. Obviously, neither the heir, nor the husband wanted the liens to attach to the property.

Fortunately, I was brought in on the transaction and was able to provide clarity on this issue. The company that I worked for at the time was able to close the transaction without the husband….and his liens!

Generally, when a person dies and leaves their property to an heir, that property is not community property (property of the spouse as well as the heir) even though we are in California, a community property state. This is usually true whether the property is left via a will, no will, trust or other method.

Now the lines can blur when a spouse inherits a property and then uses community funds to maintain the property, pay property taxes, mortgage payments, etc. Over years the property could become community property. However, in this case that had not happened so we were able to close without having to pay the husband's liens.

The heir or executer/administrator has liens...do they attach to the property?

Before I describe the following scenarios, it is important that we all understand how liens, judgments and other encumbrances attach to real property. Most of us already understand that encumbrances like mortgage loans, lines of credit or city/county liens and abatements attach to a property by being recorded directly against the property's legal description. Therefore, if I obtain a loan on 123 Main Street, the loan is recorded against the legal description of 123 Main Street.

Personal liens attach to property differently. Personal liens are recorded against the debtor's name in the county where their real property is located. Once recorded, and as long as those liens are still valid they will attach to any and ALL properties the person takes title to within that county. This even applies if the person takes title to a property for only a moment and then is removed from the property. With this understanding, we can clearly discuss a couple of different scenarios.

Recently, I opened a transaction on a newly listed probate property. The administrator had a very large private party lien for over $50,000 as well as a tax lien against his name. He was quite concerned that his liens would attach to the real property if he took title as administrator of the estate. After the conversation with me, his concerns were calmed.

The administrator or executor of an estate acts on behalf of the estate in a fiduciary responsibility. The property is not theirs and therefore, their liens do not attach to property for which they are administrator or executor. This is true even if they take title to the property as administrator/executor. Note...I said if they take title as administrator/executor. If however, they were to take title as an individual (and I'm not sure why they would unless the administration of the estate were over), their liens would attach to the property.

Similarly, the liens of an heir do not attach to a property. If an estate is selling a property, the liens of the heirs do not have to be paid during the sale of the property. However, if the heir puts a property in their name, their liens would attach to the property.

For example, in a transaction that I closed several years ago, the estate distributed the property to the heirs first, and then the heirs sold the property. One of the heirs had several liens including a child support lien, tax liens and judgments. Once he took title to the property, his liens attached and therefore had to be paid off in the sale transaction. For this reason, many heirs choose to have the estate sell the property rather than to take title in their names and then sell the property as individuals.

Glossary

To help understand some of the confusing terms used when discussing trusts, probate, and wills we have provided some definitions. All information is deemed reliable, but not guaranteed.

AB Trust- This is a trust designed to take advantage of the personal estate tax exemption, which is currently at 5.43 million dollars. It also allows the surviving spouse use of the assets, no matter what, for the remainder of his or her life.

Administrator- This person is appointed by the court to manage and oversee the court process for the estate of a deceased person or "decedent" who has died without leaving a will.

Attorney-in-Fact- This person is designated to act as an agent for the executor of a power of attorney document.

Basic Will- The basic will is designed to give everything to the spouse, if living, or the children who are 18 or above.

Beneficiary- The beneficiary is the person who receives property or other assets from a will, insurance policy, or contract.

Durable Power of Attorney for Health Care- This is a written document that gives someone the power to make medical decisions for another person in case that person becomes incapacitated in some way.

Durable Power of Attorney for Property- This is a written document that gives someone the power to make property and financial related decisions for a person who has become incapacitated in some way.

Estate- The property and assets of an individual, including all real estate, bank accounts, life insurance policies, stocks, bonds and personal property.

Executor- The person or persons named in the will who will manage the estate of the decedent. He or she will inventory all properties, pay off debts and taxes, then distribute any remaining assets to the beneficiaries and heirs.

Fiduciary- The trustee who is identified in a trust, or an institution or person who is legally responsible for the distribution, management, or investment of funds or other assets of another person or entity.

Grantor- The person who gives assets to another, usually by way of a trust.

Heir-The person legally entitled to the property of another upon that person's death.

Inter Vivos Trust- A trust created while a person is still living that holds property in trust for the benefit of someone.

Intestate- When someone dies without a will.

Joint Tenancy with Right of Survivorship- This term refers to co-owning property. When one owner dies, the other owner is legally entitled to take possession of the property, no matter what the will says.

Living Trust- This is a trust that is established during a person's lifetime in which they place property.

Living Will- The document that outlines a person's wishes in regards to life sustainment treatment should he or she become terminally ill or in a vegetative state.

Marital Deduction- A deduction set up by the government that allows one spouse to leave his or her estate directly to his or her spouse upon death without having to pay gift or estate taxes.

Pour-Over Will- Everything is distributed into a trust by this type of will.

Probate- The process in court of reviewing, legitimizing, and processing claims against a will, or in the case of no will, settling the estate according to inheritance laws.

Trust- A written document that provides for property being held by someone for someone else.

Testate- When a person dies having a will.

Trustee- The person named in a trust who manages and distributes the property for and to the beneficiary.

Will- A legal document that states how property and assets will be distributed upon a person's death.

Resources and Sources

California Land Title Association

www.ProbateRealEstateSales101.com

www.ProbateTitle.com

www.Google.com

www.thefreedictionary.com

www.probateexperts.net

www.courts.ca.gov

www.ca-trusts.com

www.CAR.org

www.Howtoprobate.com

http://www.lawlink.com/research/caselevel3/70497

http://smallestates.uslegal.com/affidavits-and-summary-administration-laws/california-small-estate-law/ (Probate Code 13100-13104, 13050)

About the Author

Kevin Sayles obtained a Bachelor of Science degree with departmental honors from the University of La Verne, Magna Cum Laude, and an MBA from the University of Redlands. He started his career in the real estate industry by working in banking beginning in 1993. While working for some of the nation's largest financial institutions, Kevin received extensive training in lending, sales, appraisals, escrow and title, and retail and commercial banking. It was there he received his introduction to both real estate closings and probate.

Kevin is a real estate investor and an expert in closing difficult transactions. Since the late 1990's, he has used his experience in the field of title insurance (real estate closing services). He has a "never say die" attitude and knows how to close the deals! It is estimated that he has closed well over 15,000 transactions while working as a title representative. He uses his knowledge and first hand experience to help close even the toughest transactions.

Currently, Kevin helps real estate agents and investors close transactions as a title representative and probate specialist.

Made in the USA
Columbia, SC
12 January 2020